THE WINNER'S CIRCLE

BY Charles Paul Conn

THE WINNER'S CIRCLE

Charles Paul Conn

Fleming H. Revell Company
Old Tappan, New Jersey

Library of Congress Cataloging in Publication Data

Conn, Charles Paul.
    The winner's circle.

      1. Amway Corporation—Biography. I. Title.
HF5439.H82C67   381   79-11428
ISBN 0-8007-0991-8

TO Phil Conn,
   the best big brother a person could have.
   Always a winner,
   and always a brother
   to love and be proud of.

Contents

Foreword

Our century-old publishing firm's interest in the Amway Corporation began with its dynamic founders, Jay Van Andel and Richard De Vos. Charles Paul Conn's interest in the amazing firm began at the same time, when he assisted Richard De Vos in writing *Believe!* which set forth De Vos's personal philosophy of living and success.

Conn, who has written ten books published by Fleming H. Revell Company, resolved to take "a candid look at Amway." The result was *The Possible Dream,* published in 1977 and called by *Publishers Weekly* "the sleeper of the year." This book appeared on numerous best-seller lists, including that of *The New York Times* (for three months), and in 1977 was rated as the sixth best-selling nonfiction book in the country by *Publishers Weekly.*

While gathering material for *The Possible Dream,* Charles Paul Conn was struck by the impact of this corporation on a half-million people who have been a part of "the World of Amway." In *The Winner's Circle* this award-winning author focuses on the men and women—and their families—who made the American Dream come true through hard work and determination, and with the help of a caring corporate body—one which takes a personal interest in them.

Charles Paul Conn's investigative reporting took him all over this country and Europe, as he interviewed dozens of

Amway figures and observed the inner workings of this dynamic organization. *The Winner's Circle* is the result of three years of research by an unbiased outsider. As publishers, we think you'll enjoy reading about real people who believe in the old-fashioned ideals of hard work and caring about each other.

THE PUBLISHERS

THE WINNER'S CIRCLE

1 On the Outside, Looking In

A free-lance writer knows a little something about a lot of things. A sportswriter is expected to understand sports; a political writer, politics; a travel writer must know faraway and exotic places; a music reviewer can't survive without knowing a cello from a viola. But the typical free-lance writer is a generalist. He is presumed to know something—at least a smattering—about almost everything. Being a knowledgeable person is his stock-in-trade.

Perhaps that is why I hated to admit that I had never heard of Amway. I am a free-lance writer, and it is the nature of the species never to admit ignorance on any subject of importance. Especially to a publisher. Publishers are the individuals who hire writers, and they expect the writers whom they hire to possess a wide (if rarely deep) awareness of all manner of things. So when this particular publisher asked me, "Do you know anything about Amway?" I brushed the question aside hastily with an unconvincing "Sure, a little"—and waited impatiently for him to get to the part of the conversation in which he would offer me an assignment. The job he wanted me to take required an understanding of Amway, he explained, and he wondered if Amway was a subject I knew something about. He wanted reassurance. So I reassured him. (Omniscience is not such a heavy burden to bear after all, especially over the telephone.)

I got the assignment. After a few weeks of dickering over such trivial details as money and deadlines, my publisher and I agreed on a deal, and signed a contract. Only afterward did I turn to the question with which the whole encounter had begun: "What do you know about Amway?" And only then did I realize that the answer lay somewhere between "nothing" and "almost nothing."

Let me state, at this point, that I was not totally dishonest with my publisher in suggesting that I "knew about" Amway. Being generous with myself—as I frequently am—I could truthfully say that I had some vague recollection of Amway, some dim sense of what it was. Certainly *Amway* had a recognizable buzz to it, as if the sound of the word triggered a feeble flicker in some remote memory cell. Somehow it evoked an almost-forgotten memory of my grandfather—long since dead and gone—selling household products from the back of his ancient Plymouth down in Georgia. But that was Watkins Products, I remembered, so that had nothing to do with Amway, but yet the association registered. And I seemed to recall that a brother-in-law had mentioned Amway to me once, and that it too had something to do with selling, but I hadn't listened and didn't remember much about it. Those were the fragments which had floated through my mind when I was asked about Amway, but now that I inspected them more closely, they didn't add up to much.

14

Not that I was alone in my ignorance. As I soon discovered, Amway was a subject about which almost everyone was vaguely aware, but almost no one had any hard information about it. On a scale of zero to ten, the knowledge of the average American adult on the subject seemed to hover somewhere between zero and one. I asked around. Most of my friends were reasonably well-informed persons, but the typical conversation went something like this:

"Ever heard of Amway?"

"Sure."

"What is it, exactly?"

Silence. Then, slowly, "I don't really remember . . . I *have* heard about it, though . . . let's see . . . that name sounds familiar . . . but I can't recall, right this minute, exactly what . . . ."

That's not what one would call a fact-packed response. (It is amazing what verbal contortions the average middle-class, college-educated person will endure to keep from uttering the simple phrase: *I don't know.*) Occasionally someone whom I asked would mumble something about Amway being "some sort of selling outfit" or "one of those transmission shops," but even then the information—or misinformation—was sketchy and unenthusiastically given.

Never, I decided, have so many known so little about so much. Unfortunately, that included me. The writing assignment which I had accepted required what the publisher had called a "working knowledge" of Amway. The job was to assist a man named Richard DeVos in preparing a book of essays on the beliefs and values of what was then being called America's Silent Majority. This man DeVos was regarded as

15

one of the nation's leading spokesmen for certain conservative social and religious values; and, for two years, the publisher had attempted to persuade him to write a book. Finally DeVos had agreed to do so, the publisher told me, and they wanted a free-lance writer to work with him, helping edit his material. That was where I came in. This man Richard DeVos was president of something called Amway, and the publisher insisted that only a writer who understood Amway could do the job properly. Understanding Richard DeVos apart from Amway was like understanding O. J. Simpson apart from football, I was told.

I didn't quite follow that logic, but I didn't quibble over it. *No problem*, I thought. *Amway is just another corporation, so what's the big deal? I'll just have them send me a copy of their annual report. I'll look over it; and, bingo! I'll understand Amway.* What could be difficult about that? It sounded dull, perhaps, but not difficult.

I was wrong. When I'm wrong, I'm usually very wrong; and this time I was definitely wrong. Understanding Amway by reading its annual report is about as easy as understanding the internal combustion machine by staring at an automobile.

As I was soon to discover . . . .

I did my job. I learned enough about Amway to meet Richard DeVos and help with his book. When it was over, I no longer had a professional reason to be interested in the "World of Amway," but I discovered that my curiosity about it had not ended when the work did. What I now knew about it had whetted, not satisfied, my appetite. What I had seen made me want to see more.

I realized that calling Amway "just another corporation" is like calling Jimmy Carter "just another South Georgia peanut farmer." There was obviously more to it than that. So I began to probe (*investigate* is perhaps too strong a word, but only barely) what I referred to as "the Amway experience." That was in 1974, and I have been at it ever since. The national news media like to talk about "the Amway Phenomenon" and, whatever that means, I have seen plenty of it, and it has never been dull. One of the skills of a free-lance writer is his ability to generate a professional excuse for indulging his personal curiosity. A writer without an assignment is, after all, just another nosy person. So I wrote a book about the Amway experience called *The Possible Dream,* which allowed me to observe and interview Amway people at all levels, and further extend what had become an enjoyable pastime under the guise of work. Through it all, I have talked to hundreds of Amway distributors (past and present), been to numerous meetings (large and small), and heard the phenomenon analyzed (intelligently and unintelligently) by countless persons, inside and outside the company.

I believe I understand the Amway World, if not perfectly, at least well enough to have reached some conclusions about it. It is perhaps important to mention that I am not an Amway distributor. There are three hundred thousand of them, but I am not among that number, nor do I have any official relationship with Amway Corporation. It could be argued that a person from inside the Amway World could make a better assessment of it than someone who, like myself, is an outsider. I doubt it. Sociologists call one who attempts to do research that way a "participant-observer," and the danger of such a

17

posture is that one gradually comes to participate more than he observes.

A music critic was once asked how he possibly could write decent concert reviews when he did not himself play a musical instrument. "My dear friend," he responded in the imperious manner of critics, "I have never laid an egg, either, but I am certainly a better judge of an omelet than any chicken on earth!" And so it is with my treatment of Amway. Any who wish to hear the opinions of an Amway distributor need only ask one; this book is written for those who would like the viewpoint of an outsider.

2 No Pigeonholes Here

My first hint of Amway's extraordinary human chemistry came in Minneapolis, where I flew one spring day to attend what was billed as a "sales rally" for distributors. It seemed a good idea, I thought, to see some of these people do whatever it is they do.

There were several surprises there for me. The first was the sheer size of the crowd. At least three thousand people filled a downtown auditorium, though this meeting was for the Minneapolis-Saint Paul area only. Then there was the tone of the meeting. Rather than the serious, strictly business atmosphere I had expected, there was an upbeat, excited air of conviviality—almost a holiday atmosphere. People were relaxed and smiling. Many of them seemed to know one another on sight, and were eager to mix and mingle. When one of the speakers said something they liked, they cheered and applauded. Loudly. Almost boisterously. The whole thing seemed natural and wholesome and—well, for want of a better word—*fun!*

A third surprise was the absence of the hard sell, the high-pressure sales pitch. I had learned by this time that Amway was a company which manufactures household and personal care products—about 150 of them—and their distributors sell these products to people in their homes. I assumed that the purpose of a sales rally was to twist every arm in the house, until the elbow joints popped. In a perverse way, I think I was looking forward to it. My anti-business biases were fairly sizable, and I thought this was going to be my first chance to see Big Business put the whip to the masses. But it never happened. I kept expecting someone from corporate headquarters to step to the microphone and bludgeon the crowd with quotas or threats and some sort of high-powered manipulation. It never came. Instead there was a slick, low-key promotional film; lots of short, snappy testimonials from distributors; recognition given to a virtually endless parade of award-winners; a highly entertaining speech on the theme of human potential. I found that I was enjoying myself despite a rather determined effort not to do so.

But the biggest surprise that night was the people, the kaleidoscopic variety of people. That was a shocker. I had expected a kind of cookie-cutter crowd—people who looked alike and sounded alike and dressed alike. And I expected them to be all straight-arrow types—Xerox copies of characters straight from a Norman Rockwell illustration. Middle America personified—that's what I expected—all middle-aged, lower-middle-class, white, Protestant, Republican, and conservative. What I anticipated was a crowd that would fit my preconceived notion of what kind of person joined businesses like Amway. Looking back, I recognize that attitude to be a thoroughly condescending one. Smug. But at that time I was so poorly informed, I had no idea that Amway people didn't fit my mold—or any other mold. I remember being amazed at how attractive (and varied) the people were at the rally that night.

Later I described them as "a small slice of America: long hair and short hair and in-between hair; business suits and blue jeans and dresses tailored, home-sewn, and off-the-rack." Many times since then I have attempted to develop a composite picture of the typical Amway distributor, and I have finally given up trying. The range of types is too broad. For every feature apparently shared in common, there are ten thousand exceptions. The Amway distributor may come from anywhere and be almost anyone. To pigeonhole all of them would simply require too many pigeonholes. That was part of my education which began that night.

I went to other meetings after that. Lots of meetings. I saw small groups of forty or fifty, big crowds of several thousand. Atlanta. Montreal. Dallas. Boston. Seattle. Small towns with names you never heard of. I heard DeVos speak; I heard Jay Van Andel, chairman of the board; often I heard people whose names I don't even remember. And always I saw those streams of distributors, speaking for themselves, sometimes in flat midwestern accents, sometimes in that soft, familiar southern drawl, sometimes with a bland California evenness. It was those speeches that I enjoyed most—the ones by the distributors—because in those speeches the remarkable Amway aura showed most clearly. Those people weren't describing a marketing system, neat and logical with lines and figures and flow charts. They were showing a little piece of themselves, lifting the lid off a corner of their lives to reveal something of their own ambitions and dreams and loyalties. Their speeches perhaps weren't designed that way, but to me

21

they disclosed an intriguing truth: that Amway was more than a business to these people—as they kept saying—that it indeed had a far richer meaning for them than that.

My suspicion at the outset had been this: that Amway people were ordinary folks out to make a buck; that the whole thing could be reduced to money, plain and simple; that Amway people were just like everyone else, only perhaps a bit more greedy. After the speeches are over and the cheering has faded, what we have here is a bunch of people who play little games with one another to pick up a few dollars—that's the way I had it figured. But, on looking more closely, I came to believe that that jaundiced view was clearly an inaccurate one.

I could see that whatever this thing was that Jay Van Andel and Rich DeVos had built, it was more than a high-toned money-making machine. It was inarguably an important force in the lives of many stable, intelligent people. Lots of people were making lots of money. No question about that. But beyond the money, they seemed genuinely to *care* about Amway and to care about each other. Not only that, but they felt good about what was happening in their lives. They felt good about themselves. *Now here,* I thought, *is a rare combination: (1) These people make money. (2) They care about each other. (3) They feel good about themselves.*

If a person really wants to understand a painting, he should talk with the artist. Want to know what makes an airplane fly? Talk to the engineer. If the meaning of a play puzzles you, talk to the playwright. And so it is with Amway. To know what it all means, the place to start is with Rich DeVos and Jay Van Andel.

3 Jay and Rich

Ask Amway distributors what the business means to them, and some colorful metaphors are offered.

"Amway is a blank check," says Vede Coleman. "You can fill it out for any amount you want, and there's always plenty of money in the bank."

"Amway is a wall socket, an electrical outlet," says Bill Campbell. "As long as you stay plugged in, you can feed off its energy and positive attitudes and inspiration."

"Amway is a big field of juicy, ripe strawberries," says Art Charlton, "and I feel like I have just one small basket. There's just so much more than we can take!"

If Amway is a blank check, a wall socket, and a strawberry patch, then surely Jay Van Andel and Rich DeVos are the Federal Reserve Bank, the Edison Power Company, and the Good Earth. They are the source of whatever Amway does and is. When the two men organized Amway Corporation in 1959, it was a product of what was already almost a twenty-year friendship. It was the residue of twenty years of creative friendship: trial and error, dreaming, working, learning. And the evolution of the business since 1959 has occurred with the careful daily attention of the two men. Amway was not originally conceived, nor is it currently operated, by committee. Rich and Jay are its source and its symbols.

Jay Van Andel and Rich DeVos are chairman of the board and president, respectively, of Amway Corporation. They own the company and all its assets outright. But they don't merely own and run it; they made it. They designed it, put the pieces together, and breathed life into it. Amway is by them, of them, and in their image.

I was once in the lobby of the Center of Free Enterprise (the company's home-office complex in Ada, Michigan), standing before the life-size portrait sculptures of the two founders. A man stood nearby, staring at the sculptures; he turned toward me and said, solemnly, "Amway *is* Rich and Jay," and without another word walked away. I had never seen the man before—or since—in my life, and I thought it a rather strange encounter, but I've reflected often on what he said. What did he mean, Amway *is* Rich and Jay? I think he may have summed up an important element of their success and the explosive growth of their company. DeVos and Van Andel not only own the company and operate it; they symbolize what is best about it. They embody its values.

What are the essential components, the most basic elements of the Amway concept? They are these ideas:

- a belief in the supremacy of individual effort
- confidence in the free-enterprise system
- a high priority on financial independence
- an emphasis on sharing with other people

There, at its most irreducible level, is what seems to me (though no one at Amway may agree) to be the core values of the Amway system.

If so, the man standing in the lobby that day was right: in a sense, Amway *is* Rich and Jay. They are flesh-and-blood examples of the most important shared values of half a million people.

First, their own personal lives comprise a success story of virtually mythic proportions. It is a towering testimony to the ability of men to rise above the commonplace by sheer force of ability and will.

Second, they are constant, articulate advocates of the free-enterprise system (along with other conservative sociopolitical viewpoints), and have committed major chunks of Amway's corporate resources to that ideological campaign.

Third, each has earned rather than inherited his personal wealth.

Fourth, they have well-deserved reputations for being personally interested in their distributors; they have learned the fine art of deflecting praise and recognition to others without seeming to do so. It is as if the constant effort to look out for the best interests of the other partner has developed in each an enlarged sensitivity to other people generally. Each is an unusually other-centered person, and that quality is reflected in the overall corporate style.

It is, in fact, this fourth quality which elicits the greatest amount of comment from Amway distributors. To be sure, distributors are aware of the founders' political views, and undoubtedly a majority of distributors agree with those views. But Amway people frequently brush aside discussion of such things to tell of some single, simple way in which Van Andel or DeVos have shown personal interest in who they are and what they are doing. There are too many such stories to discount them lightly; everyone who has been around a few years has an anecdote to tell, a little snip of a story, a vignette that reveals a warm, personal side of these two men whom they so greatly admire.

Alistair Cooke once wrote, "You can meet some people thirty, forty times down the years, and they remain amiable bystanders. Conversely, you can meet some other people once or twice and they remain permanent influences on your life." Van Andel and DeVos seem to fall in the latter category for hundreds of people. Among them is a young distributor from Virginia, who told me that his greatest experience in Amway had come at a travel seminar in Hawaii, when Van Andel sat down beside him on the beach, knew his name, and asked how he could help him with his business. "Can you imagine the chairman of the board of a half-billion-dollar company caring that much?" he asked me. Among them is a couple in Saskatoon, Saskatchewan, who told about the handwritten reply their ten-year-old daughter received after writing a "fan letter" to DeVos. And the distributor for whom Van Andel painted a picture of what he thought she could accomplish—gently, patiently describing for her the things he believed she would achieve; or the distributor couple who still haven't forgotten that, thirteen years ago, they phoned DeVos when they were in trouble, and he "did us a personal favor that almost literally saved our lives." People who haven't forgotten in thirteen years aren't likely to forget—ever.

What all of this begins to resemble is hero worship. In a

way, I suppose, it is. But it is hero worship in its purest and finest sense—an admiration for those who embody the qualities which one finds most important. Certainly it is not the cloying, mindless hero worship of the sort that rock singers or movie stars elicit from pubescent teenyboppers. Some writers have attempted to make it that; they cruise into a single Amway rally, see the excitement which Van Andel or DeVos generates, and rush to their typewriters to describe, in derisive terms, what one reporter called the "godlike reverence" which Amway distributors have for the two founders. This is sheer nonsense. These are not blubbering teenagers, these Amway distributors, but intelligent, competent adult men and women. Their enthusiasm for Van Andel and DeVos issues from an awareness that these two men could have walked away from the pressures of leadership long ago, wealthy and sated—but, instead, have chosen to stay, to work, to lead, and to divert to the distributors the enormous rewards of their system. And these people have seen their own lives better because of it. So of course they stand and cheer and applaud when Van Andel or DeVos comes on stage. Under the circumstances, that seems an entirely appropriate gesture.

The problem with discussing Van Andel and DeVos as symbols is that it tends to obscure the more important element of their extraordinary success—and that is the partnership, the synthesis, the interplay by which their friendship has survived and their careers flourished. They dance a remarkable *pas de deux*. Like light and shadow, they define one another, constantly shifting roles without changing the overall pattern.

Much is made of the dissimilarities of the two men—so much, in fact, that many people fail to observe that similarities

27

are there, as well. When I first met the two men, I was struck, as most people are, with the obvious differences between them. The contrasts are virtually an Amway cliché: Mr. Inside and Mr. Outside, the "people man" and the "systems man," the thinker and the doer. But as I spent more time with each man, and looked past the clichés, I came to see that the two men are much more alike than not. Their contrasts are largely of style. The traits they share in common, on the other hand, are of substance—the things that matter in the long run: each is extremely well disciplined; each is strongly committed to the other; each is supremely self-confident, even if he expresses it differently. Each is ambitious to the hilt, not personally, perhaps, but for the company and the Amway image. Each believes deeply in the old-fashioned Calvinist virtues, and each is absorbed in the challenge of keeping Amway on track and moving full ahead.

"To have a problem in common is much like love," the great playwright Tennessee Williams said, "and that kind of love was often the bread that we broke among us." So, it seems, is the bond that holds Van Andel and DeVos together. The "problem in common" is the ongoing effort to make Amway what they want it to be, what they feel it has the potential to become. That is the great common love which they share, and which trivializes all the smaller differences and contrasts. I often hear people who, having observed the very different styles of the two men, marvel at their ability to work together so closely in spite of these contrasts. Such people miss the point. The much greater miracle is that two men so similarly disposed, at the core, should have found

28

each other so early in life, and had the good sense to recognize each other as brothers under the skin. That they did, and that each possessed such bottomless wells of raw ability, is a miracle of chance or "fate." It is catching lightning in a bottle, not to be duplicated or even understood, but only marveled at.

4 An Undertaker and a Metallurgist

It would be a mistake to be so dazzled by DeVos and Van Andel that one forgets to ask the crucial question: do Amway distributors—the ones out there selling the products—really make any money? History is replete with examples of armies in which the generals eat ruffed grouse and caviar, while the soldiers up front in the trenches starve, poor fellows.

Amway is a business. Like any other business, it must be measured by its ability to make money for those who do its work. And not just a trickle of money, either. To live up to its reputation, Amway must deliver a sizable financial return to that distributor who makes an honest investment of his time and effort. As I studied the Amway sales and marketing plan, three questions emerged in my mind: first, *can people make money in Amway;* second, *can people make a* lot *of money in Amway;* third, *can a* lot *of people make a lot of money in Amway?*

Amway distributors earn money in a variety of ways, primarily through retail sales of products and bonuses from the corporation. The cleverly designed Amway system allows a distributor to sponsor other, new distributors and be paid bonuses from the corporate treasury as the new distributor is successful. What that all means is that an ambitious distributor can potentially make lots of money—perhaps even a full-time income—through a combination of selling products, recruiting (called sponsoring) new distributors, and teaching them the business and supplying them with products. (*Editor's note:* A more detailed explanation of how the system works appears in the Glossary at the end of the book. Readers who are not acquainted with the system and terminology should read that brief section before continuing.)

Naturally, one may engage in these activities with whatever degree of involvement he chooses. The company makes no rules governing the amount of time the distributor commits, and consequently an individual's involvement might range from full time to very-very-very-part-time. Most people begin Amway as a part-time job to earn a second income, doing the work in the evenings and on weekends. Much of the appeal of the system, as opposed to other more conventional part-time jobs, is that the distributors have the choice of working as much or as little as they like, when they like, and be paid accordingly.

There is also the tantalizing elasticity of the business, its potential to stretch into something far larger and more lucrative than just a part-time income. Who knows? It could happen. One thing for sure—there's never any "big money" if you're making your part-time dollars stacking boxes in a warehouse for five bucks an hour. A year from now, you'll still be stacking those boxes for that same five bucks. No elasticity. In the Amway plan, one can spend the same amount of time selling and sponsoring, make the same immediate money as if he were a part-time hourly employee, and have some prospect of a substantially larger income developing.

That's the way it works on paper. But does it ever happen that way in real life?

It has been said that a giant once picked up the entire United States, turned it up on one corner, shook it vigorously, and everything that was loose fell down into Southern California. For some reason, I always think of that when I fly into any city in that part of the state.

Like San Diego, for example. San Diego is, among other things, the home of Dennis and Kay Beecher, who are Crowns in the Amway award hierarchy. Dennis is tall and wears his dark, gray-flecked hair in tight, short curls—which sounds worse than it looks; Kay is stylish and attractive. They are a striking couple. Dennis Beecher does not look or act like your friendly neighborhood undertaker, but in fact he was just that, and quite a good one, apparently (I'm not sure how such things are judged), until a few years ago. Before Amway. He no longer pursues that profession for the simple reason that one doesn't ordinarily do that sort of thing, unless he needs the money—which the Beechers no longer do. Since Amway.

Dennis got into his profession early, working a summer at his uncle's mortuary in Kansas. After college, he attended the University of California at Berkeley to earn a master's degree in mortuary science. Soon afterward, in 1963, he and Kay moved to Oceanside, California, he to work as a mortician, she, as a dental assistant and technician. Dennis was ambi-

33

tious, and during the ten years on the job in Oceanside, he advanced to the position of executive secretary and general manager of a group of four mortuaries. "We were success-oriented," he says, "but for many years all of our ambition was tied to the mortuary business. I eventually began to feel that it was never going to work out for me to become president of that company and really control the thing, so by 1971 I was getting a little frustrated."

So was Kay. She quit work to have the Beecher's first child (Debbie), and after a year-and-a-half at home with her, she was "looking for something." Life was long on tedium and short on fulfillment. The pattern was set: housework and church; housework and church. "Life was pretty narrow; Dennis was very busy with a career I couldn't share, and I was searching for something. I wasn't sure what."

When Kay saw a presentation of the Amway plan, she borrowed some cassette tapes of rally speeches, brought them home to listen to them, and immediately got excited about the possibilities. Not Dennis. Kay thought about it more and decided this was surely the thing for them. Not Dennis. So Kay did it alone. For three months she worked at building a distributorship, and eventually Dennis became interested and agreed to help. He explains why: "Things kept adding up. For instance, we had seven people killed in an auto accident on the way home from Disneyland one day, and I had to go tell the father. That day, the importance of a man's time really crashed in on me. I kept talking to widows who said, 'He just retired, and then he died just when we were going to have time together.' I thought about that, and how common it was, and thought maybe Amway could keep that from occurring."

So Kay's business became the family's business. The early growth was slow. "We would get frustrated during those first couple of years, because we weren't growing as fast as we wanted. But we didn't back off. We went at it all the time; that was our style. We always had both oars in the water." It took the Beechers two years to become Ruby Direct Distributors. Dennis resigned his job in 1973, when his Amway income grew as large as his mortician's salary. "We weren't getting rich in those first few years," he says, "but we were making a good living and we could see the big money coming. In our mortuary business, we had invested one hundred eighty thousand dollars, and it took seven years to get the first net gain from it, so we were accustomed to the idea of working now and getting the big rewards later."

And, sure enough, it has happened just that way: Pearl, Emerald, and Diamond in 1974; Double in '76; Triple in '77; Crown in '78. For the first two or three years, as the Beechers describe it, they "worked eight days a week, twenty-five hours a day. We didn't take a vacation, watch TV, nothing. Now we don't work nearly as hard as we did, and our income and production are ten times greater. We paid our dues. We stuck with it. We really believed in it, so we poured ourselves into it. And now it's really paying off! Not only for us, but for so many of the people who are working with us. Some young friends of ours, Bill and Beth Vogel, are already Double Diamonds at the ages of twenty-seven and twenty-five. This thing *works!*"

"Okay. You're making money," I say. "But are you making a *lot* of money?"

Dennis Beecher isn't embarrassed by the question. (People

35

with lots of money rarely are.) "Look around you," he smiles back at me, "and answer that question for yourself."

So I look around me. We are in Rancho Santa Fe, San Diego's most exclusive residential area. I have read somewhere that homes start at about three hundred thousand dollars here. Bob Hope has a home here; Robert Mitchum has one; so does Dennis Beecher. I look around the house: fifty-two hundred square feet, soaring ceilings, indoor pool. Outside is a horse ring and stable area, right next to where the tennis court is going in. I had seen a 1931 classic Ford Phaeton in the driveway, right next to that new Lincoln Continental. I remembered how hard it had been to schedule the interview, what with the Beechers on vacation in places like Europe and Lake Tahoe and their mountain cottage so much of the time.

"Amway has given us a new way of life," they say. "It has put us in the league, financially, that we want to be in. We live in the neighborhood of our choice; drive the cars of our choice. Debbie goes to the school of our choice and so will our two sons [Kit, four; Davey, two]. Amway has given us more time for balanced living in all areas of our life, and time to help others, as we never could before."

The late Hank Williams, master of the mournful country song, used to enjoy saying, "Don't ever worry about anything, because nothing's going to turn out right anyhow."

That's how Pat and Betty Kaufmann felt in early 1972, when after thirteen months in the Amway business, their total sales volume was only six hundred dollars. Pat was an engineer, a metallurgist who did zirconium research (zirconium is a metal, not a disease) for a large company in Albany,

Oregon. Betty was assistant chief medical technologist at a local hospital. Pat was an expert in his narrow field of zirconium isotropy, and he enjoyed his work. The Kaufmanns had only one problem, and it was that everlasting problem of not enough money. Never enough money. Healthy income matched by healthy outflow—the old leaky bucket syndrome.

Pat frequently went to the YMCA in Albany during his lunch break to jog with a friend. His jogging partner, another metallurgist, asked him one day to take a look at a new business he had started. Out of sheer friendship—and perhaps not to lose a jogging partner—Pat finally went to see the Amway plan. He and Betty started their distributorship with visions of making a thousand dollars a month extra income, but after over a year in the business, they were making only a tenth of that amount. So they talked about quitting. Betty remembers: "We had a long, straight talk about it. Finally I looked him in the eye and said, 'Are you sure you really want to do this thing?' And we decided yes we did. So we went back to work. After that we didn't sit around thinking about what we didn't have. We knew we had what it took, to be whatever we wanted to be, whenever we were willing to pay the price."

Within another year, the Kaufmanns were making that thousand dollars a month, qualifying as Gold and Ruby Directs the same month. As the new money poured in, their life-style reflected it. First it was Betty who resigned her job at the hospital, as her salary became less important to them. Then for a two-year period, Pat had his engineering salary held in escrow for him by the company. For that two years he didn't cash a single paycheck, a way of demonstrating to himself that the Amway money was indeed large enough to support them. He hardly missed it. Finally he called it quits entirely, drew his two years of accumulated salary, and resigned to work his distributorship full time. "The corporate environment became limiting," he explains. "There were just too many things I wanted to do with my time to continue working an eight-to-five day when I didn't need the money." The Kaufmanns, still in their thirties, became Diamonds in 1977.

"This business has made an enormous difference in our lives," Pat says. "We work hard, sure, but it's the kind of work that we take a lot of pleasure in. It's a rewarding kind of work. I get the same satisfaction from doing a good meeting that I might otherwise get from sinking a putt or jogging fifty miles a week. The kind of things we do in this business can be that pleasurable."

"But haven't you given up a lot—like playing golf or skiing on weekends—to achieve what you've achieved in Amway?"

"Well, no, not really. We still do the things we enjoy, only we do them at a higher level of quality, for shorter durations. For example, we used to ski thirty days a year, always at places around here, places which aren't the best. Now we see ourselves skiing two weeks a year in Switzerland or the other Alps, or some place that's really tops. Or, instead of playing golf every weekend on a little public course, we're building the kind of income that we can fly to Scotland or Pebble Beach or Doral and play the really great golf courses of the world. Higher quality—shorter duration."

Is the money really that good?

Pat Kaufmann does not hesitate. "Let me describe it this way. The last year I worked as an engineer, I was saving my entire paycheck, my wife was not working, I drove a Mercedes 450 SL, we took vacations all over, from Hawaii to the Caribbean, and I bought several major pieces of investment real estate. During one particular week recently, our total cash income during that one week (which included some annual bonuses) was greater than our combined salaries for an entire year before we got into the business."

He didn't have to draw me a picture.

5 Horatio Alger Revisited

As everyone knows, "The rich get richer and the poor get poorer." I'm not sure exactly what this means; but I have heard so many people say it, that it seems impossible for it not to be correct. The first person who taught me this was my grandfather, who didn't explain it either, but said it with such authority that I have never questioned it. I recall that he was displeased with this state of affairs, being poor himself and not eager to become more so. I recall also that he blamed this condition vaguely on the Republicans (whom he blamed for almost everything, being a Georgia Democrat).

Conventional wisdom has it that professional people, wealthy people, college-educated people—in short, people with at least a moderate level of social status—have advantages that others do not have. Life does have a certain momentum, and those who are succeeding in one arena seem to succeed more easily in another. The obverse of this is also true: People in debt tend to stay that way. In the words of another old folk axiom, "It *takes* money to *make* money." Or, even more succinctly: "Them that has, gets." All of which

41

adds up to a rather discouraging world to the have-nots.

If the much-heralded "Amway opportunity" is no different from this pattern, it is really not such an exceptional deal after all. There is nothing new about people with money making money, or people who are successful in one enterprise being successful in another. It is appropriate to applaud persons such as the Beechers and the Kaufmans, but in each case a middle-class couple with considerable professional success demonstrated their ability to succeed, once again, in another area. That is all well and good, but it is hardly surprising. It appears to be true that hundreds of engineers, lawyers, dentists, businessmen, college professors, and assorted professional persons are able to make the Amway system work for them. But what about the have-nots, the down-and-outers, the men and women without college degrees and suburban homes and friends in the country club? What about the guy who is still looking for that first big break, who is willing to work for it, but who must start from absolute zero? Isn't that the classic, gold-plated, rags-to-riches, up-from-nothing, old-fashioned American Dream? Find an opportunity where that can still happen, and you've found something worth shouting about.

Ron Hale is a large man, about six feet four inches, 240 pounds, who wears a size 14EEE shoe. He and his wife, Toby, grew up together, childhood friends and schoolmates, in Virginia. There is a Virginia of lush valleys and prosperous farms—the Virginia known for southern charm and gentility. But there is another Virginia, too, the harsh Appalachian coal-mining country of southwestern Virginia, where life can be bleak, and hope is a rare commodity. The mountains around Russell County, where Ron and Toby Hale grew up, are beautiful mountains; but people can't eat scenery, or dress their kids in it, or trade it in for a college education or a new coat when winter comes.

When Ron finished high school, he took the same ticket out of Russell County that so many young men from the mountains take—Uncle Sam's ticket. He joined the United States Air Force in 1957. There were no jobs except in the coal mines; and he had no money for college. He saw an air-force recruiting ad on television and made his decision in thirty seconds. A week later he signed up and was gone. Soon after enlisting, Ron reluctantly accepted the idea of a lifetime career in the military. "I was pretty well convinced the outside world was no place to be," he says, "and the air force was the best deal I was ever going to find."

He and Toby lived the transient life of the career soldier. They lived in Texas, England, France, Missouri, and Virginia, with a fifteen-month tour of duty in Goose Bay, Labrador, for Ron alone, sandwiched in. Three children were born in those years and, while they were not altogether bad years, they were increasingly frustrating ones. Ron, with no college education, found himself stuck at lower ranks and lower pay, consistently receiving undesirable assignments because of his lack of training. He was passed over for promotions which he had been promised, and which he felt he deserved. His problems were exaggerated by his own shyness and sense of inferiority. "I was brought up in a part of the country where people weren't very friendly," he says, "and I never learned how to talk to other people comfortably. I began to realize that I was a grown man, and I didn't have any friends because I didn't know how to make friends. I was just a big mountain kid who had no confidence in himself and wasn't developing any."

He was also broke. Low pay and a family of five—not a good combination. He couldn't get a part-time job, because his service job required him to work twenty-four hours on and twenty-four hours off. They lived in the cheapest available housing and got along the best they could. "I remember Toby used to go out and hang the diapers on the clothesline in the wintertime, wearing tennis shoes. I'd look out the window at her, and get such a hopeless feeling I'd just die inside. It takes something out of a man not to be able to provide for his wife any better than that."

In 1968 the sensitive Ron Hale suffered what was to him a final humiliation: "Our old fifty-seven car quit. It absolutely quit and wouldn't go anymore. I had to have some sort of transportation, but we didn't have a dollar to our names. So for the first time in my life—after eleven years of marriage—I had to call home and borrow money for a car. That broke me inside. One of my buddies had been trying to get me interested in Amway, and that's when I started listening. When you have to come down off something you've been proud of and stuck to for years, it hurts a man inside."

The Hales were living in Portsmouth, Virginia, at the time. Once they started, they made a 100 percent commitment to making the new business work. "We had no other way," Toby says. "It was this or nothing. This became our whole lives, and we realized that people in Amway were more concerned with what we did after we got in than what we had been before. We knew that those people really cared—that we had as good a chance for recognition as anybody. At last we were doing something where we were on an equal footing with everyone else." The Hales' Amway friends helped them believe in themselves. "My sponsor," Ron reflects fondly, "was the first person I ever met who put his arm around me and said to me, 'Ron, *you* can do it.' "

The magic worked. They were making money. "Ron and I slept on a rollaway bed, and he could never stretch out completely on it. I hadn't had a new winter coat since we were married. On that first Christmas I took the Amway money and got me a cloth coat with a fur collar, and a king-size bed for Ron. Those were our first major purchases with Amway money." They became Direct Distributors within thirteen months, and Toby literally jumped up and down in excitement when the telegram came from Ada making it official. By then they were making a much larger income from Amway than from the air force, and a year later he retired from the service.

"I remember driving out of the air-force base on my last day, looking back at the gate guard, and saying 'No more!' I was so tired of having no control over my life." They moved afterwards to Kingsport, Tennessee, where they now live and work as Diamond Directs, with a lovely home, swimming pool, Cadillacs, diamond jewelry for Toby, and all the other symbols of the Good Life. Their years of financial struggle are firmly behind them.

Despite their newly won affluence, the Hales seem still to enjoy working with people from "our own background. We haven't forgotten where we came from," says Ron, "and we enjoy offering this business to people like ourselves. We can relate to them. Our first Direct only had a fourth-grade education, and could hardly read or write. But he's a terrific distributor, and we love working with him. We get real satisfaction from knowing that we can communicate with those people, and that we've had a lot to do with their success.''

From the coal camps to the factory towns, being broke is the same everywhere.

Clare and Shirley Gunnett. She is irrepressible, outgoing, a whirlwind of movement and personality; he is by contrast quieter and more restrained, though not without his own sense of humor. They grew up in Kalamazoo, Michigan, and built their Amway business there.

They met at the "midnight movie" at a local theatre, and married when he was nineteen and she was fifteen years old. Clare has always been a worker, a man with great pride that he can provide for his own family and make his own way. Even when it wasn't easy, he always managed, because there is something strong and solid inside men like Clare Gunnett. They are true to their own sense of honor, and that includes doing what must be done to pay the bills. The Gunnetts had four children by 1963. Clare had gone to work at a paper mill when he got married, and thirteen years later he was still there, working sixty to seventy hours a week. For three years he had worked without a single day off.

Shirley, too, knew how to work. "I had a real thing about supporting my family," Clare says, "and I didn't want her to work, because we had young kids at home." But that didn't keep her from trying, sometimes with disastrous results. She opened a country-style restaurant called the Northside

Lunch. It was a total wipeout, closing with no net profit and bad bills—twenty-seven of them—strewn all over town. She tried selling rosebushes door-to-door, picking up discarded plants from a nursery, putting foil around them, and peddling them around the neighborhood. It was another no-profit venture.

Therefore, when Shirley saw the Amway opportunity and signed up in late 1963, Clare was not only uncooperative, he was downright unpleasant about it. He stormed, he raged, he threatened to leave her. "I'm still working overtime to pay off the bills from your last business," he reminded her grimly. "We can't afford another one of your crazy ideas."

Shirley Gunnett did not get where she is today by being unintelligent. She recognized that she had to do something—fast—to convince her husband that this new business was more promising than her previous ones. "When I see the money you're making, I'll get in with you," he had promised. So to the bank she went, and borrowed three hundred dollars on a ninety-day note. She took the money, bought a batch of new clothes, a modest inventory of Amway products, and two chintzy white French Provincial chairs (fifty dollars each), which she placed in the front room of their scruffy little house. And she waited for Clare to return from work.

He came in the door that night: blue jeans, T-shirt with cigarettes rolled up in his sleeve, greased-down hair. He spotted the two chairs.

"Where'd these come from?"

"I bought them with my Amway money."

He was suspicious. "Well, I'd better not get a bill for this stuff!"

"Don't worry, you won't. I paid cash for every bit of it."

That got his attention. *Cash,* she said! It was a flimflam right out of Laurel and Hardy, but it got his attention. *If she paid cash for all this stuff,* he said to himself, *maybe there's money in this Amway thing after all.* So he took a closer, more open-minded look at the Amway plan, and not long afterward joined Shirley in the business.

They were an aggressive combination. He would go out, find prospects, and bring them home to Shirley, who explained the Amway sales and marketing plan to them. They sponsored many people that way. (It was a year after they had become Direct Distributors before Clare showed the plan for the first time.) In January of 1964, after only two months of activity, they became Direct Distributors, and Clare resigned the job at Sutherland Paper Company that had been his bread and butter for his entire adult life.

Was the new business sturdy enough to replace that regular wage earner's paycheck? Words are cheap, but numbers do not lie. Here are the numbers, straight from the Gunnett's tax returns: 1963, total wages, Sutherland Paper Company, $7,839.42; 1964, total income, Amway distributorship, $36,489.85.

That was only the beginning. The Gunnetts have progressed steadily through the Amway award and income levels in the past fifteen years, and now are Triple Diamond distributors. They live in the style which one would expect of successful, high-income businesspersons. It is all there, all the creature comforts, the investments, and the sense of security that money and accomplishment bring. And surely, fifteen years ago, no one would have predicted it for the Gunnetts but the Gunnetts themselves.

George Eliot, the British author, once wrote: "It seems to me we can never give up longing and wishing while we are thoroughly alive. There are certain things we feel to be beautiful and good, and we must hunger after them." Clare Gunnett once said a similar thing. He said it, I believe, for himself, and for the Hales, and for hundreds more like them: "We had a driving force to succeed in this business that I absolutely cannot explain. We knew inside us that we had to have it, and we didn't stop until it was ours."

6 A Widow and Walkaway Incomes

So the money was there, I decided.

It became difficult to argue that point. After meeting dozens of Amway distributors across the country, it was clear that (1) people *could* make money in Amway; (2) people could make a *lot* of money in Amway; and (3) a *lot* of people could make a lot of money in Amway. The money was there to be earned—no doubt about it.

But was the money stable?

Was Amway a business that must be constantly pushed, if it is to move at all? *Okay,* I thought, *I see that people can make big money in Amway; but maybe all the talk of "dreaming" and "believing" obscures the fact that Amway is just another job. Maybe it is just another arrangement in which one puts in his hours and collects his paycheck, with no real hope of establishing an income that can continue after the day-to-day grind stops.*

As long as a distributor stays healthy and energetic, I figured, Amway works. But does the Amway system have the capacity to absorb change—even drastic change—which occurs in the distributor's life? Good income, yes—but is Amway the kind of business that can provide *permanent* income?

I was still asking myself that question when I met Bernice Hansen.

Bernice Hansen is a widow, a vigorous sixty-seven-year-old who lives near Grand Rapids. She is short and lively, with the friendly roundish face of the perfect American grandmother. She and her late husband, Fred, were original Amway distributors when the corporation was formed in 1959. Fred had been a barber in Grand Rapids before moving to Akron, Ohio. Rich DeVos came personally to Akron to get them started in the business in the early days, and within two years they had become successful enough to make a full-time income from their distributorship.

In many ways, they were a typical Middle-American family, this quiet former barber and his wife and three daughters. They became Diamonds in the Amway pin system, with a large, steady income and a position of popularity and influence among the nation's Amway distributors. He was the breadwinner, the leader of the family; she was his partner, working in all the ways that the conventional wife-and-mother role called for. Theirs was a stable, successful Amway home.

And then came Fred's heart attack. July 6, 1968. He was placed immediately into the hospital's intensive care unit and stayed there five-and-a-half weeks. During those forty days, there was time for Fred and Bernice to talk, plenty of time to rehash the good times they had had, the struggles, the successes—and the uncertain future which lay ahead. Most of all, there was time to talk about the business.

"We knew Fred's condition was serious," Bernice recalls, "and we talked about it. We talked about the futility of barbering, about how much more hopeful the Amway business had been. We had built the business together, and Fred had a great deal of pride in what we had. Toward the end, he told me, 'You're just going to have to carry it on. Will you do it?'

"I got my three daughters together and I told them, 'We're the women in Fred Hansen's life, and we're going to put his business over the top.'" Fred Hansen died on August 15. When he died, a family friend called to express condolences, and asked that question every new widow hears so often: "What in the world are you going to do now?" But the concern was unnecessary. "The women in his life," as Bernice had so affectionately called them, went to work; the business continued to grow; the family income never faltered. Because of the structure of the Amway business, the family's material life-style did not change.

The Hansen distributorship reached the Double Diamond level in 1970, Triple in 1974, and Crown in May of 1975. Marianne (the oldest daughter), Sue (who married Skip Ross, then a Direct Distributor from California), and Karen (who with husband Jim Hussey now works at Amway corporate headquarters)—all shared in the effort and the excitement of seeing their dad's business go "over the top." Bernice says that she and her daughters never thought about quitting. "I had never even shown the marketing plan before Fred's death," she explains, "but I learned fast. Of course I do things differently than if Fred were still here. Skip and Sue are my partners now, and he usually shows the plan; but when I show it, I always call it 'the business Fred and I built.'

"We place a bit more emphasis on women in our business. We have an executive women's club, with morning meetings and a luncheon every month. We give the housewives lots of recognition. I just love this business. I love sharing it with other people. Once you make your livelihood, at my age, the rest of the money is not so important. I pay too many taxes now! But I love to see other people meet their goals. A couple of years ago we went with ninety-two of our distributors to Hawaii for two weeks, and some of them had never even been on a plane before! That's the kind of sharing that makes this business unique."

Back in the 1950s, when Fred Hansen first decided to give "this new business" a try, it seemed a risky, potentially unstable income for a family man. He told his wife then, "Just give me one year to try it. If it doesn't work, we'll go back to Grand Rapids and barbering." Fred never went back to barbering. The business worked, and kept right on working ever since, not only for him, but for the women in his life, long after he was gone.

The Hansen story is a lesson in the potential permanence of an individual Amway distributorship. It reveals not only the pluck of a remarkable woman, but also the staying power of the Amway income. It underscores the resilience of the system, its capacity to absorb change and upheaval in the life of a distributor without folding. There are hundreds more such cases in which the business has survived, even buffered, various kinds of stress.

Dick Lowe, a Diamond from Philadelphia, tells of being hospitalized while on an Amway trip in California. The problem was diagnosed as a pinched nerve in his neck. For three months he was unable to touch his business, and his income did not slip a single dollar. Fred Sanborn, a California Diamond, suffered an illness that would have deflated most family pocketbooks. He took a trip with his wife, Jan, to Acapulco, and came home with a case of infectious hepatitis. He was unable to work for almost a year, but during that year maintained an income from his distributorship of over three thousand dollars per month.

In Colorado, an Emerald Direct had been in the gas-station business before becoming an Amway distributor. He recently had two brain tumors removed by surgery over a period of three years, once lying unconscious for almost three months. He came out of the coma inquiring about how the family bills were to be covered, and was told that everything was being paid from his Amway income. "Without this business," he says, "I would have been totally wiped out. In fact, my business grew while I was hospitalized."

Fred Blechman, another California Direct, tells a similar story. His wife developed terminal cancer a few years ago, and "as her health declined, so did our involvement in the business. Selma's death was an emotional blow I couldn't handle. I went into virtual retirement, opening my office only four hours a week and having very little to do with my business. I turned down speaking requests; I withdrew from group activities. My sorrow turned somewhat to bitterness. However, I had taken care of my business for a number of years, and now my business was taking care of me. The fact that the Amway business plan continues to provide benefits from past efforts means that my income has stayed high, while I have struggled to get on my feet again emotionally. I have continued to receive an income in excess of my former salary as an engineer! Last year, for example, although my inactivity began two years before, I received fifty-one hundred dollars in annual bonuses alone.''

One unusual example is that of Dusty and Betty Owens, who are Double Diamonds in Tampa, Florida. Dusty, formerly a professional entertainer, is a popular person in the Tampa Bay area. He is a friendly, open individual whom people seem to like automatically. Politically, he is a committed conservative Republican, and in 1976 ran as the Republican nominee for a seat in the United States Congress.

The campaign was a long, difficult one which required Dusty's full-time involvement for several months. The eighteen-hour days of vote seeking left no time at all to spend on their Amway business. Through that time, the Owenses' income continued, without interruption, at the high level they have enjoyed for many years. Dusty lost the election, but he made an important political impact in that area—and, along the way, provided a unique example of the "staying power of Amway income."

Not all the examples of this durability of Amway income involve sickness or death. Frequently, less traumatic events interrupt the lives of distributors without interrupting their profit. Numerous distributors have spent periods of several months out of the country—or even moved permanently to foreign countries—and still maintained healthy incomes at home base in the United States. Some have taken extended sabbaticals or moved residences to pursue special hobbies or projects, living off the continuing remuneration that is inherent in the Amway marketing plan.

All of this sounds too good to be true, of course, because it has a bit of the something-for-nothing ring to it. That was my reaction when I first heard the claim that Amway could provide a hardworking distributor with "walkaway income." *That just couldn't be so,* I reasoned. How could it be possible for a company to pay a man during a period of time when he isn't actually on the job, producing? But when I checked the stories out, they proved to be true, and gradually I realized the basic inconsistency of my skepticism—for a writer, of all people, to question the existence of "walkaway income" is an inconsistency bordering on absurdity. People who make their living writing books survive on that kind of income. Midnight oil at the typewriter now means royalty income years later. Long after the work is done, the money keeps coming in. I wrote books in 1971 and 1972 that still yield checks from my publishers in 1979. That is not a rip-off; that's not something-for-nothing; that is simply the way the profession is structured: Work very hard now, and keep reaping the profits into the future.

The opportunity for that kind of income is what the Amway structure offers its distributors. Wayne Walker, a Texas distributor, says it best. "I knew a guy down in Texas who owned some natural gas wells," he says, "and that man told me that every month he gets a check for eight thousand dollars as a royalty off that gas well. That's what I call 'walkaway income.' You don't have to be there looking after it every minute for it to produce. That's the way people get paid for writing a song, or writing a book, or inventing a new gadget. I wanted that kind of royalty-type income. Amway came along and gave me an opportunity to use my skills to do that. I couldn't write a book or a song, and I couldn't accumulate the capital to drill an oil well; but in Amway I can still use my skills and my hard work to build an income that will keep on coming!"

And, indeed, why not?

That concept somehow makes the Amway success stories I had been hearing less magical, and hence more credible. It makes good sense, after all, that if a man creates something that continues to produce, he should continue to share in its profits. That is accepted without question for those who create books or songs or coal mines or inventions or movies. Why not for the man who creates an Amway business, a marketing organization? Why not permanent, walkaway income for that kind of honest effort, too?

With that concept in mind, the whole Amway thing, with all those people making all that money, seems quite logical.

7 Momentum

I have trouble believing in things I can't touch.

I am embarrassed to admit to such a primitive form of cynicism, but it is true nevertheless. You can describe something to me and get my attention, but before I believe it's real, I want to touch it and see it with my own eyes, preferably up close. Nobody likes to be razzle-dazzled, like a country boy at the fair. That goes double for writers. Writers wrap their skepticism around themselves like a protective blanket—perhaps because they know, better than most, that words can be pretty insubstantial things sometimes. Speeches, interviews, annual reports—all are made of words and feelings, and those can be the biggest razzle-dazzlers of all.

At some point, a writer wants to look at something more substantial than words and feelings. That time came—time to go to Ada, Michigan, and try to find something solid, something I could touch.

I went, I saw, and I touched. What I saw was an entirely different facet of the Amway story, a side of Amway that bore little resemblance to the talk of dreams and sharing and recycled lives that I was hearing so often from Amway distributors. This Amway was streamlined, superefficient, no-nonsense industrial production at its best. The best equipment, the best computers, the best technicians, the most modern facilities. This was high-speed machinery kicking out aerosol cans at the rate of four per second; platoons of chemists bending over charts and test tubes in quality-control laboratories; tractor trailer rigs streaming in and out of warehouse loading docks. Half-a-billion dollars' worth of business means massive stockpiles of raw materials, three hundred acres of buildings, parking lots, and storage facilities. It means a one-million-gallon water treatment plant just to keep up with daily operation.

Is Amway substantial? What is more substantial than a building? Amway owns dozens of them, including massive Regional Distribution Centers all across the country, adding up to 2½ million square feet under roof. Want something about Amway you can touch? Try a BAC-111 airliner (Amway has two of them) or a 116-foot diesel yacht (they dock it in Fort Lauderdale) or a cherry tree (Amway owns groves of them in Puerto Rico).

The point is that Amway is not just an "experience"; it is also a corporation with major facilities, holdings, and widely diversified activity all over the country. To fuel the system that makes possible all those distributors' dreams, there must be a hard-nosed team of manufacturing and distribution experts constantly at work. It takes a lot of people—thirty-four hundred of them—to make the products and supply the services and keep the records and ship the products. (And write the checks. Don't forget: write the checks!) I already knew that, of course, when I traveled to Ada for the first time. But still it was extremely impressive to see it all in operation, a facility and work force much larger and more sophisticated than I had expected, buzzing with constant motion and an almost palpable sense of momentum. It is difficult to walk around in the bowels of that enormous place and not be reassured that believing in Amway is not being razzle-dazzled, after all.

The growth of Amway Corporation, from where it began twenty years ago, is an impressive accomplishment. That early history is by now well known to most observers of recent American business history: Van Andel and DeVos organized the company in their basements in 1959, and originally housed the entire operation in a forty-by-sixty-foot converted gas station. The first year's estimated sales volume barely reached half-a-million dollars. To call the growth over the past twenty years "explosive" would hardly be an exaggeration. The more interesting part of Amway history, in fact, might well be in the future, as the rate of growth in the past three years is higher than at any similar period in the past. *Amway's growth in the past three years has equalled its growth for the entire seventeen-year period preceding.* That is particularly impressive when one considers that, three years ago, the company was already gaining national attention as a phenomenally fast-growing corporation. There is no indication that a plateau has been reached, and the most dramatic stories may be yet unwritten.

An explanation of Amway's performance lies not only in the distributor force, but also in the corporate staff who keep the wheels turning at home base. "The bigger this thing gets,"

says Rich DeVos, "the easier it is to run, because we have so
many capable people around here doing the work. We have a
superb staff in virtually every area. They handle the day-to-
day operation, and Jay and I get involved only at the major
policy level."

That disclaimer notwithstanding, the two founder-owners
stay impressively well-informed about the goings-on at Ada,
as well as on the field, and the influence of their personal,
informal styles affects the entire operation. Amway maintains
all the usual employee activities found in any large corporation—an in-house magazine, recreational programs, and so
on—but seems to maintain a high level of employee morale
that cannot be attributed to these conventional practices. This
may be a result of the emphasis placed by DeVos and Van
Andel on personal communication with employees, regardless
of their position—or lack of it—in the corporate pecking order.

Part of that emphasis is an ongoing series of meetings in
which employees come to the auditorium or boardroom of the
Center of Free Enterprise to participate in face-to-face
dialogue with one of the founders. I attended one of those
sessions once, and was amazed to see the manner in which
Rich DeVos discussed the state of affairs in Amway with a
small crowd of employees. The group included production-
line workers, secretaries, executives, all sitting together in a
single egalitarian mass. No social stratification in that
meeting—the button-down-collar boys and the little old ladies
off the assembly lines neither intimidated nor deferred to one
another. Attache cases and lunch buckets stood side by side
that day.

When De Vos began to field questions from the group, he got mostly complaints. Small, niggling complaints. But he answered each one as if it were an issue of major concern. I jotted some notes:

> man asks why hamburger pattie without bun costs same as with bun. RDV sends sec'y to find out. Woman complains, no diet drinks in machine. RDV says will fix. Same woman: jello too bland in cafeteria. RDV says no can fix. Older man asks why not more compensation for 2nd and 3rd shifts. Explanation given. Man says parking lot gates not opened far enough to let cars in at start of day. RDV tells jr exec to check it out.

And so on. I was fascinated at the sight of the president and co-owner of a half-billion-dollar corporation standing there, treating each question seriously, and taking the time to answer personally the questions of his hourly-wage employees. It showed me something about the Amway style. It indicated the degree to which these two men, who preach the respectability of the individual so forcefully on the field, practice it so consistently at the home base.

People ask me from time to time, "Why is Amway growing so fast?" and I always reply, "That's simple." (This is always a useful response when one doesn't know the answer to a question. It gives him longer to concoct an answer. The more difficult the question, the more effective it is to respond in this manner, as it puts the questioner on the defensive, and makes the eventual answer seem coherent, even if it makes little sense at all, which is usually the case.)

"That's simple," I reply. "Amway is growing so rapidly because it has momentum."

I often wonder exactly what I mean by that. I feel that it is essentially correct, but "momentum" is a difficult thing to define. Roughly, a company has *momentum* when it keeps doing things better and better, and people are noticing more and more.

Amway has momentum. Talking to veteran distributors, one can almost feel it. Over and over again, longtime Amway distributors have told me that building the business is becoming easier; that they are making more money; that their businesses are operating more smoothly with less hassle; that, to paraphrase an old line, "Every day, in every way, things are getting better and better." Corporate figures show not only the rate of growth is increasing, but that the amount of money earned by the average distributor is growing as well.

What are the sources of these impressively healthy vital signs—this vigorous momentum?

(1) *A growing public visibility.* Amway is becoming more and more highly visible in the American marketplace. The company has economic clout, and it is using it. In 1977, the corporation bought the Mutual Broadcasting System—lock, stock, and microphones. Mutual is the largest network of affiliated radio stations in the world, with eight hundred affiliated stations across the country. To further solidify its foothold in the radio market, Amway has completed negotiations to purchase WCFL in Chicago, a 50,000-watt, clear-channel station which one broadcasting figure in Chicago told me was the "sleeping giant" in the entire midwestern broadcasting industry. Plans

were recently announced to acquire the services of a WESTAR I communications satellite, parked in a stationary orbit 22,000 miles above the equator, and 500 small earth stations, to modernize the Mutual operation, as well as to provide future communication links for Amway's worldwide business.

Amway has also purchased the Pantlind Hotel in Grand Rapids, Michigan, a 750-room hotel which has been a landmark in that city for 64 years. The hotel will be renovated and operated by a non-Amway management team. (Amway is the largest user of hotel facilities in Western Michigan, using hotel space for distributors visiting its Ada facilities.)

An important part of the company's higher level of public visibility is the activities of Van Andel and De Vos. Both men are devoting what seem to be larger amounts of time to activities which gain favorable notice for Amway in the general public. Van Andel is the chairman of the Chamber of Commerce of the United States, one of the most prestigious national positions in the American business community. De Vos serves on the board of directors of the National Association of Manufacturers. Both are active in other political, civic, and religious affairs. Newspapers, magazines, and columnists are increasingly doing major stories on De Vos and Van Andel, and the corporation itself, and the tone of these articles is shifting markedly from one of caution or outright skepticism to a more favorable one.

(2) *A reputation for integrity*. In the direct-sales industry, where products reach the public through distributors who are largely volunteers, a company is only as good as its reputation

for integrity. That type of reputation must be built slowly, over a period of years. It is the kind of thing which comes with time, as a company proves itself to an inherently skeptical public. Amway has done that by consistently behaving responsibly—even generously—toward its own distributors, with the ripple effect of that integrity reaching eventually to the general public.

Dale and Shirley Dawson, now Diamonds in California, are among the many distributors who told me of some single incident of such corporate behavior. He was a military pilot in the U.S. Air Force when they entered the business and moved to Hawaii. "The first thing we did, when we got off the boat, was to go look in the phone book to see if there were any Amway distributors there." There were no Directs on the Island of Oahu, where the Dawsons lived, and they found themselves to be starting the business in what was virtually a new territory for Amway.

Problems arose. Shipping problems. The Dawsons' orders of products, shipped in small lots from Michigan, were constantly delayed on the docks in Honolulu by labor disputes there. They improvised, and were growing anyway, reaching volume of twenty-two thousand dollars within four months after arriving. But then disaster shoved its head over the horizon—disaster in the form of a major dockworkers' strike, which was projected to begin several weeks later. "We saw it coming, and could do absolutely nothing about it," Shirley recalls. "We had worked so hard, and there was no doubt that the docks would be closed down completely. It would literally wipe us out."

As luck would have, Rich DeVos made a refueling stop in Honolulu on a flight to the Fiji Islands. The Dawsons went to the airport to visit, and they mentioned their fears to him. Soon afterward the Dawsons were in Ada, and a company official met them with a question: "Do you think you guys could find a place for a warehouse in Hawaii, to stockpile products during the dock strike?"

Can a frog jump?

"Sure, we can!" said the Dawsons.

"Well, we realize you have a special situation there, and we are shipping one hundred thousand dollars' worth of products to Hawaii. Find a warehouse for it, and it'll see you through the strike. Good luck."

The Dawsons found a warehouse, the products arrived and were stored, and three days later the dockworkers walked off the job, completely closing down the waterfront for a long, bitter strike. But the Dawsons and their distributors had products, and their growth—and income—never stopped. "There was no profit to Amway in Hawaii for a long time," the Dawsons say, "but for one little group of distributors they made all that effort, and put all that money on the line."

That kind of corporate spirit communicates. It communicates integrity and generosity to its distributors, and they in turn communicate it to their customers and prospects. Nobody writes magazine articles about it. No newspaper puts it in the headlines. "There ain't no news in being good," said an Irish writer.

No, but it registers with the people who count most. And they do not forget it. Their conviction of Amway's goodness, based as it is on a twenty-year history of such incidents as the Dawson one, builds and rises and becomes an irresistible force.

That's called *momentum,* and it takes a few years to build it, and Amway has it.

8 Through Different Eyes

If two men see the same thing differently, it is because they look through different eyes.

When a woman walks into a roomful of strangers, the dentist in the crowd notices her teeth; the cosmetologist looks at her hair; the fashion designer observes the dress she is wearing; the English teacher is especially aware of her diction; and, if she is pretty enough, every unmarried male in the room looks to see if she is wearing a wedding band.

Everyone has his own unique experience of the world he lives in, and that includes the world of Amway. Some experience it with more intensity of feeling or with fresher meaning than others; but all experience it through the filter of their own unique perspectives. As I traveled and talked to Amway people, heard them speak in giant rallies and small coffee-table conversations, saw them paint their own individual pictures of Amway, I was impressed with the variety of perspective, the different visions of Amway which emerged. The steelworker sees in the Amway fabric different threads from those seen by the physician or the housewife. For the inquiring outsider, like me, these constantly shifting descriptions of Amway were fascinating. Everyone, it seems, analyzes Amway in terms of his own instincts or occupational training, and there is something to learn from all of them. Some stand out more than others: the people-oriented approach of a former public administrator; the systems analysis of an engineer; and the psychological interpretations of a young California psychiatrist.

The former public administrator is Bill Britt, a North Carolinian who spent several years as a city manager in that state before going full time as an Amway distributor. Bill and his wife, Peggy, are Double Diamonds who live in Chapel Hill. He is in his late forties and has an insatiable appetite for work. He enjoys talking about the business, analyzing it, breaking it down to its barest parts for closer scrutiny, constantly inspecting the evidence of his own distributorship to see what makes it tick. In his virtually endless preoccupation with Amway, one thing emerges in all his conclusions: to Bill Britt, the Amway business is all about people; people with dreams and desires; people who for some reason have the will to change things in their lives. Britt sees the Amway business as a people business.

Bill Britt grew up poor. His father had a drinking problem, Bill says, and that means the entire family—he was the oldest of eight children—had a money problem. "What did you want to be when you were a kid?" I asked Bill. "I wanted to not be poor," he answered. So he had a series of spare-time jobs as a child. That's how he approached life even then. Problems were generally people problems, he figured, and the solutions were generally people solutions.

70

At the age of eleven, he bought his mother a piano, and went to work to pay for it, sacking up groceries at the A & P food store in Hampton Roads, Virginia. "I wanted to bring some happiness in her life," he explains. He had a morning paper route, an afternoon paper route, and worked at A & P in between. After high school, he joined the army, hoping it would give him a chance at a college education when he got out. He worked hard, went to Officers Candidate School, and wound up in Korea, building bridges and putting in minefields. He left after three years at the rank of first lieutenant.

Back home, Britt enrolled in North Carolina State University and worked his way through by building houses. After graduation, he entered public service, working first as an assistant city manager in Raleigh, then to Sanford and finally to Goldsboro. Along the way he found time for a master's degree in public administration, and was serving as city manager when he was shown the Amway opportunity.

"I wanted to have the extra income to be a truly independent city manager, so I was looking for a second-income career. After I got in, the first nineteen people I tried to sponsor turned it down flat. I was new at this and I didn't know how to get somebody's attention. I didn't know much about the business, but I had been working for years with people, and I knew something about people. It didn't take me long to realize that if you show this thing like a salesman showing a vacuum cleaner or something, that prospects think you need them more than they need you. That's not the way to show it. After I figured that out, we started rolling." Indeed they did. The Britt volume hit $8,400 the third month, $15,400 the fifth month.

Today, Britt has a coast-to-coast organization, conducts massive rallies and weekend conventions for distributors in his group, and is inarguably one of Amway's most productive and influential leaders. His philosophy of business is simple: "The more you help other people get what they want, the more you get what you want." He preaches a doctrine of any-man-can-do-it, and emphatically sweeps aside the suggestion that professional or well-educated persons find the Amway business easier.

"In this business, you're not looking for a person of a certain age or occupation or background. You're looking for the dreamer. You're looking for the guy who knows what it is to be down, and he's sick and tired of it. All he wants is a chance, and he's ready to work for it. That's the guy you're looking for. Forget the label; forget the college degree; forget the occupation. Look at the person. The only requirements for a person to succeed in Amway are: one, does he have a body temperature; and, two, does he have an undeniable dream? It will never be difficult for me to relate to the little guy. The more money I make, the greater my sense of responsibility is to show it to other people."

Britt pauses, lowers the volume of his voice a notch, leans back in his chair. "Yeah, I guess I do get pretty intense sometimes," he smiles. "But Amway means a lot to me. It's changed me. I used to love things and use people. Now I've learned to love people and use things. I've seen wonderful things happen to lots of people, since I came into this business, and I think that's what Amway is all about. Amway is people working together and sharing together and making good things happen in our lives."

To Bill Britt, Amway is a people business.

Bob McKann is a former engineer from Houston. He fits the stereotypic pattern of the professional engineer: calm, cool, collected—and thoroughly analytical. He is a systems man. He believes in orderly systems, reliable ones, systems that work.

McKann's training in naval architecture during World War II led him to a fifteen-year stint in hydrodynamic research, working with high-speed experimental aircraft, then to a top-level position with NASA, the nation's space agency. He was a project engineer during the glamour years of the American manned-space program, monitoring spacecraft instrumentation during numerous Redstone, Mercury, and Apollo missions. He was introduced to Amway in 1966, and four years later resigned his twenty-five-thousand-dollar-per-year NASA job to do the business full time. He and his wife, Betty, maintain an active distributorship in Houston, and have never regretted the move away from what he describes as the "pressure cooker" atmosphere of the space program.

I visited Bob McKann in Texas one day and asked what, to him, was the remarkable thing about Amway. Given his slide-rule background, the reply was perhaps to be expected: "To me, Amway is a beautifully designed system. It's amazing, really. The thing that impresses me most about it is its excellent design." Isn't it somewhat unusual, I asked, to describe the Amway business so coolly, in such a detached way, when it is more often described in terms of the more intangible things, like dreams and freedom and enthusiasm?

"Well, of course not," he responded. "Certainly those

73

emotional things are there, but Amway works, in the final analysis, because it is such a perfectly designed system. Rich and Jay themselves obviously took a very systematic approach to this thing. Something with this kind of balance doesn't just happen."

Has he ever used his engineering skills in the business? "Sure. When we started, I plotted the projected growth curves of our sales volume, drew it all out on charts the way it ought to work, and it was really reassuring to see it happen that way. It was reassuring to see that it responded to an orderly design.

"The genius of the Amway design is that you have a very clear means of evaluating performance. It's called *PV*. It's that simple. All else flows from that. If a man isn't earning, it's because he isn't producing, and he knows it. So many other systems have ambiguous ways of evaluating performance and deciding who gets compensated for what. Even NASA has that problem. NASA's system creates a highly stressful atmosphere—works great for putting men on the moon, but it's very destructive to the people involved. Amway, very simply, has a better-designed system."

When Bob McKann looks at Amway, he sees a marvel of design, an impressive engineering accomplishment. The eye sees what it is trained to see, and nowhere in America is there a better-trained engineer than Bob McKann.

I thought I had heard all the possible analyses of Amway, after a couple of years of asking distributors for their perceptions of the business. I was sitting in an Amway meeting one day, idly listening to the flow of words from a lineup of Direct

Distributors who were taking turns at the microphone. Unexpectedly, a statement caught my attention. "The thing I see in Amway," a young man was saying, "is that it is the most effective means I have seen by which people can gain power over the *negative space* in their lives." *What an unusual thing to say,* I thought. Nobody talks that way, except a psychiatrist. So I asked someone who he was and what he did. And sure enough . . . .

Gary Bonnell is a psychiatrist in private practice in Santa Rosa, California, a town of seventy-five thousand people, an hour's drive north of San Francisco. An M.D. graduate from George Washington University, with his psychiatric residency at the Cleveland Clinic in Cleveland, Ohio, Dr. Bonnell came into Amway, as most professionals do, to develop a backup income. I asked him what he had meant by Amway's overcoming "negative space."

"In my practice," he explained, "I constantly deal with people who are really struggling with negative images of themselves. This is a serious struggle, and most of them never find a way to gain power over that negative self-concept. Amway is an incredibly effective environment in which people can do that. It not only gives a kind of positive-thinking mental set—lots of things do that—but, more importantly, it combines that with a reward system simultaneously. People not only *tell* themselves they can succeed at something, but they have a way of seeing the tangible evidence of it in Amway's reward system. It can be a powerful combination."

I wondered if Dr. Bonnell ever shows the business to his clients. "Well, yes, on a few occasions, but only if I have some other relationship with them apart from the doctor-

75

patient relationship. Actually, I'd like to show it to more of them, but I have an ethical code in that area, and I'm careful not to violate it. Lots of them could use the Amway business—not financially, I mean, but emotionally. A lot of people I work with are having problems primarily because of low self-esteem and no opportunity to taste success. The business could give many of them the power to break out of that trap."

Dr. Bonnell says he saw this therapeutic quality in Amway the first time he heard about the business. He was shown the plan by a friend who had entered Amway since the last time the two had visited. "When he showed up, I could hardly believe it was the same guy. There had been a literal transformation in his character structure and in his self-image. It was a tremendous change, and I was amazed by it. It was obvious that whatever Amway was, it had given him a different emotional outlook, so of course I was curious to know more about it. That's what I mean by 'gaining power over your negative space.' That's really what Amway is all about!"

To Gary Bonnell, it is. Just as to Bob McKann and Bill Britt it is something else entirely. If two men see a thing differently, it is because they look through different eyes.

It is a mark of the richness of the Amway experience that it evokes such diverse analyses from so many intelligent people. Whatever else Amway is, I concluded long ago, it is always interesting. No one ever complained of boredom in the World of Amway.

9 Winners Never Quit

How does one tell about Tom Hanson?

One could talk about his quick, flashing smile, and those beautiful teeth. Or say that he was a short man—about 5'7"—with a strong, muscular body. That he was balding on top without being embarrassed about it.

But those things do not describe Tom Hanson; they merely tell how he looked. Those things you can see in a picture. Knowing about the real Tom Hanson—the man on the inside—requires meeting him, talking to him, and seeing that enormous vitality he always had. One cannot do that anymore, because Tom is dead, and those who knew him are left to describe him, using words and pictures as best they can.

He would be the first to tell you that the most important part of his life—and the best part—was the last six years. He died at the age of twenty-nine, and by then he had already become a big winner in the World of Amway. He and his wife, Debbie, earned their Double Diamond pins in November 1977, the month he died. He was one of the young tigers of the Amway distributor force, already very successful at an early age, with no indication that he was any less hungry or less eager to work and build than on the day he got into the business.

Tom and Debbie are from western Pennsylvania, both from working-class families, both ambitious but without big dreams when they met. "We weren't poor, but we had to work for everything we had," Debbie says. Tom was a student at Indiana University of Pennsylvania; Debbie was in a nursing school nearby. After they married and both had graduated, they moved to Smethport, Pennsylvania. They went to work, he as a teacher and wrestling coach at Smethport Elementary School, she as a nurse on the medical-surgery floor of the Bradford Hospital twenty-five miles away. They lived in a trailer, and every day Tom walked to school, while she drove their red VW back and forth to work. They had just settled into that routine, when a friend invited them to a "business opportunity" meeting in the basement of a local elementary school. That night they signed up as Amway distributors. It was March 1971.

Debbie remembers: "Tom wanted the business from the beginning. I figured if he wanted to do it, it was all right with me. He was always into something even before Amway; just teaching and coaching were never enough for him. He had tried selling snowmobiles and insurance. He was always aggressive, always had lots of drive, but it wasn't always directed properly, and he was frustrated because he just wasn't doing all that he felt he should do. He didn't like the fact that I had to work. I enjoyed the nursing part of it, but the long drive, working different shifts and weekends, not seeing much of Tom—none of that I liked—and I wanted to quit and start a family. Tom was always looking for something he could do to replace my income, so I could stay home.

"In March we got into Amway, and I got pregnant and quit work. Our business grew right from the beginning. Tom was great at it. He was so friendly, so open; he could talk to anyone. His standard opener was a simple question: 'Are you making all the money you want to make?' And then he would go from there. He talked to all his old college and high-school friends, people who worked there in the Quaker State oil fields with his dad, and people he met around town. He loved it. The baby came in December. Tom was showing the plan in a meeting forty miles away that night, when I felt that it was time for me to go in. I called him at the meeting, and he told me to try to wait until he got home, because he had the car, and it was twenty-five miles to the hospital. At 1:00 A.M. we headed toward Bradford; he wore his coach's stopwatch around his neck and timed my contractions all the way. Well, he got me there on time, and we named our son Aaron."

The Hansons became Direct Distributors three months after starting their business, and within a year and a half went full time. Tom resigned his teaching job, sold the little trailer, and moved his family to State College, Pennsylvania, a town the Hansons selected simply because "we could live anywhere we chose, and it's such a lovely town to live in—not too large, not too small." In the years from 1973 to 1977 their business boomed. They built Amway groups all over Pennsylvania, and in Maryland, New York, and other neighboring states. They passed the Emerald level; became Diamonds, and set their sights for Double Diamond. "When we decided to go for Diamond," Debbie remembers, "I said to Tom,

79

'Okay, you just tell me what you want me to do, and I'll do it.' He told me, 'Honey, just take care of the kids and give me the freedom to work. I want us to go straight on up to Double Diamond, then we'll relax and enjoy it.' "

Double Diamond came in November 1977.

But Tom never got to wear the pin. He had an appointment to work with a group of his distributors on Wednesday night, November 24, the night before Thanksgiving. The group was in Salisbury, Maryland, and Tom flew down in his private plane, a six-place Piper Seneca II, which he had bought as both a reward and a tool of his Amway business.

"Tom always wanted to fly," explains Debbie. "We lived four miles from an airport, and he was going out there and taking lessons before I even knew it. One of the Directs in our group is a commercial pilot with Allegheny Airlines; he helped teach Tom, and checked him out in a twin-engine. Tom was a good pilot. We had just bought the plane; it was barely a month old. That was Tom's dream, that plane. It was really beautiful, and it had over thirty thousand dollars of radio equipment in it. We used the call letters 777TD—that stands for Tom and Debbie."

Tom flew to Salisbury alone that afternoon; but the weather deteriorated in the late afternoon, and by the time he got to Salisbury, he couldn't land because the fog was too bad. After flying two hours alone, he had to turn around and fly all the way back. He tried to land at two places along the way, but couldn't get clearance because of the fog. He decided to land at the Lewiston Airport, so he called a friend on the plane's telephone and asked the friend to meet him there. He hoped to be back home in State College by 9:00 P.M. The friend drove to the airport, heard 777TD on his radio as the plane approached the landing strip, then lost radio contact. The plane apparently came over the field at about two hundred feet, off the runway, turned to make a second approach, and crashed into the mountains in the fog.

It was her closest Amway friends who brought Debbie the news that night, ringing her doorbell at about midnight. "I *knew* as soon as I opened the door," she says. "They told me the plane hadn't been found yet, and maybe there was hope, but I knew he was dead. I said, 'Let me be the one to tell the children; we're not going to get hysterical around here.' So I did, and then I got dressed and the people started coming." The funeral was that Sunday, and over two thousand people came to honor Tom.

Today, more than a year later, Debbie lives with her three children (Aaron is now seven; Alicia is five; Aleta, three) in a wealthy Pittsburgh suburb. She is a very pretty twenty-nine-year-old woman, with the small features and high cheek-bones of a model. She wears a gold heart on a slender chain around her neck, with a single diamond mounted inside the heart. She moves her hands constantly, expressively, ticking off points on her fingers as she talks:

"It hasn't been an easy year, but I realize how much I have to be thankful for. Tom left us a very secure income when he died, and it's the kind of income that will keep right on going. In fact, our business has grown in the last year, even though I'm just now getting things settled down so that I can work it again. I guess the first thing a woman usually worries about, with a young family like I have, is *where the money is coming from—how are we going to get along?* Well, Tom saw to it that we don't have to worry about that. If it weren't for this business, I would be going to work as a nurse every day at some hospital somewhere, trying to find someone to keep the kids, so I could make a living."

She fingers the diamond at her throat, looks out the window, and goes on softly: "My whole goal when we got into the business wasn't to have lots of money, but to be a wife to Tom and a mother to the kids. That sounds 'Pollyanna,' but it's true. I've never been overly impressed with the big houses and diamonds and that sort of thing. Tom provided me with lots of that and I thought it was great, but that's not what I was in it for. I just wanted to see Tom succeed because I knew he wanted it so much. I saw the Amway business change Tom. It made him so much more positive, gave him such a better attitude about things. It gave him a chance to be a winner, to have people respect him, and that was the biggest thing for him, even more than the pins and the money.

"I remember, when we first started, we were young and didn't have any money; we didn't have a car; we didn't have any clothes. And we approached people who at that time had a lot more money and success than we did. One successful businessman that we showed it to wouldn't even hear Tom out. He told us it was *repugnant* and we were *repugnant*. That was the word he used. And I remember sitting there, and Tom was trying to show the man that it was on the level. I couldn't take it any longer and I got up and left. Tom came after me a few minutes later. But that was the night Tom's attitude really changed. He refused to be intimidated. After that, when some guy started giving him a rough time, he would say. 'Look, I'm giving you a business opportunity, so either accept it or don't accept it but don't give *me* a rough time!' One thing for sure, Tom wasn't a quitter. He believed in what he was doing, and he wouldn't let anyone take it away from him.

"Tom always said, 'For every adversity there is a seed for equal or greater benefit.' And he believed that. That's the kind of thing the business gave him—that kind of belief and positive attitude. So I'm trying to keep that spirit, now that this has happened. I keep thinking about that statement and telling myself it must be true, because Tom said it."

Debbie's friends and Amway business associates are eager to tell of her poise and courage during the year and a half since Tom's death. Only two weeks after the funeral, she flew to Washington, D.C., to speak to a crowd of over three thousand Amway distributors, fulfilling a long-standing commitment of Tom's. She is now conducting the business herself, running her large organization, continuing to build what she and Tom had begun together. She has an amazing resilience, a tough courage which, though she will not acknowledge it, is there nevertheless. She insists that she is merely doing "what anyone else would do" in her situation.

"Me, brave? I'm not brave. People talk about how brave I am—they just don't know. They just aren't around me in those times when I'm scared. I'm not brave. This is all an unknown thing to me and I'm scared most of the time. Is it difficult? Sure, it's difficult. Everything I do without Tom is difficult. But no matter what happens, I know I'll survive. When Tom died, everything in my life changed. But I've proved myself to myself, and now I know I can handle this business."

A slogan hung on the wall above Tom's desk, and when she

moved to Pittsburgh, Debbie took it with her to put on her office wall there. It is a quotation from Vince Lombardi:

WINNING IS NOT A SOMETIME THING; IT IS AN ALL-TIME THING. YOU DON'T WIN ONCE IN A WHILE: YOU DON'T DO THINGS RIGHT ONCE IN A WHILE: YOU DO THEM RIGHT ALL THE TIME.

That is the spirit that Tom Hanson communicated to those who knew him. It is the spirit that made him one of Amway's most successful leaders at the age of twenty-nine, and without question it lives on in Debbie. The first thing she did after the funeral was go to meet with the distributors who had expected to see Tom on that night before Thanksgiving. "That's where he was going when he died," she explains, "and I wanted to go there and talk to those people and make sure they didn't feel badly about it.

"My main motivation right now is to do right by my Amway group and be a good mother and a good example to my kids. Tom built this business for those three kids, and I'm going to do whatever is necessary to maintain it for them. We loved Tom, and I'm so glad he loved us enough to build a business for us. I'm so glad that when other men would have quit, Tom didn't quit."

Rich DeVos and Jay Van Andel, friends since their high-school days, share the duties of "chief executive officers" at Amway. They founded the corporation in 1959, and still personally manage its operations. *Below:* Amway distributors "sponsor" other persons in the business. The sales and marketing plan is often explained by use of a chalkboard presentation. Here Chuck Strehli of Texas "shows the plan."

Performance Bonus Schedule:	
7,500 or more points	25%
6,000 to 7,499 points	23%
4,000 to 5,999 points	21%
2,500 to 3,999 points	18%
1,500 to 2,499 points	15%
1,000 to 1,499 points	12%
600 to 999 points	9%
300 to 599 points	6%
100 to 299 points	3%
Less than 100 points	0%

$$6 \times \$100 = \$4,200$$
$$\times \ 12 \times \$100 = \$8,400$$
$$12 \times \$200 = \$28,800$$
$$12 \times \$300 = \$52,600$$
$$12 \times \$400 = \$96,000$$

Amway's home base is Ada, Michigan, near Grand Rapids. Its manufacturing facilities, shown here, sprawl over a 300-acre site, with over a million square feet under roof. *Below:* New Direct Distributors are welcomed to a training seminar at the Center of Free Enterprise by a reception line of corporate officials.

A constant stream of visitors see the Amway plant in specially de-signed tour vehicles. *Below:* California Double Diamonds Dave and Carol Kendall tour the computer center during their VIP tour of the Amway plant.

The Amway incentive system includes seminars to various parts of the world for high levels of achievement. Here a group of distributors try their luck on skis at Lake Tahoe. *Below:* Distributors who reach a high level of success are called Diamonds, and become members of the Amway Diamond Club. New members traditionally make a speech at their first meeting of the club. Here Mel and Bea Behnke of Kansas City continue that tradition.

Crown Direct Distributors Jerry and Sharyn Webb of Texas at a recent Diamond Club meeting. *Below:* Triple Diamond Distributors Rick and SueLynn Setzer of South Carolina share their Amway experiences with the audience at a recent convention.

The Sanborn Singers is a professional song-and-dance troupe comprised entirely of Amway distributors. The group performs at many Amway events across the country each year. Here the troupe rehearses. *Below:* A curtain call for the Sanborn Singers.

The January 1979 meeting of the Diamond Club, shown here at San Diego's La Costa Country Club, included over 250 distributors. *Below:* Conventions and mass meetings are frequently conducted by the corporation for its distributors. Here is a typical crowd at a recent convention in California.

From Utah, Leo and Amy Grant joined Amway in 1974. They were the first of seventeen Direct Distributors in their hometown of twenty-six thousand. *Below:* Frank and Betty Lou Miura were Amway's first Diamond Direct Distributors from Hawaii. Here they are pictured at a recent Amway convention.

Crown Directs Michel and Cecile Chapdelaine of Quebec accept a
pencil portrait of themselves from an Amway artist, during the
Chapdelaine Day at Ada, which celebrated their achievement of
Double Diamond status. *Below:* Canada's first Crown Ambassadors
(Amway's highest award) were Jim and Sharon Janz, shown here at
a corporate seminar in Maui, Hawaii.

West Germany's booming Amway business is spearheaded by couples such as Peter and Eva Mueller-Meerkatz, shown here with their family at their home in Augsburg. *Below:* Tom and Debbie Hanson are pictured at a meeting of their organization in the summer of 1977. Tom, whose story is told in chapter 9, died in November of 1977.

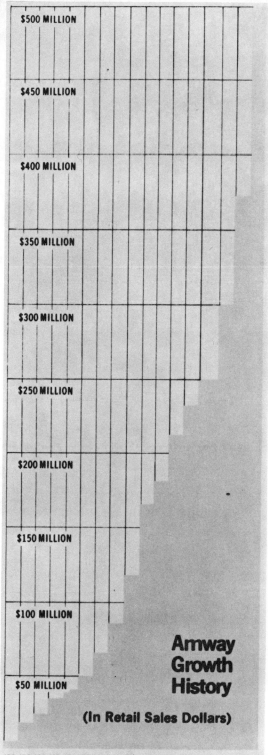

Amway Growth History

(In Retail Sales Dollars)

$500 MILLION

$450 MILLION

$400 MILLION

$350 MILLION

$300 MILLION

$250 MILLION

$200 MILLION

$150 MILLION

$100 MILLION

$50 MILLION

'60 '63 '64 '65 '66 '67 '68 '69 '70 '71 '72 '73 '74 '75 '76 '77 '78

Amway's dramatic twenty-year growth record is graphically displayed in this chart, which shows annual estimated retail sales (in millions of dollars).

The Center of Free Enterprise, which houses the executive offices of Amway Corporation.

Richard M. DeVos, president of Amway Corporation, is a director of the National Association of Manufacturers.

Jay Van Andel, chairman of the board of Amway Corporation, and national chairman of the Chamber of Commerce of the United States.

10 All in the Family

Family. For many people, that's what life finally comes down to. The wife or husband, the children—the family. It is probably more important to more people than any other aspect of life.

According to the experts, the family is in trouble. In modern America, the average family is caught in the crunch by a constantly rising cost of living. The traditional pattern of *one* breadwinner working at *one* job to support *one* family is proving inadequate in millions of cases. The most common way to solve that problem has been for the wife to go to work, usually not because she wants to, but because two paychecks are needed to pay the bills. "I really don't want some day-care worker to raise my children," says one young working mother, "but what else can I do? Unless I work, there just isn't enough money to go around." Increasingly, mothers are going to work, and family life is usually the loser.

A different way to beat the money crunch is for the father to hold two jobs. According to the U.S. Department of Labor, 600,000 Americans took second jobs last year for the first time, an increase which brings the number of persons holding two jobs to 4.6 million, an all-time record. That trend puts pressure on the traditional family relationships, taking parents away from home and their children for a larger proportion of time.

Amway was perhaps not designed to be a family business, but it has become one in a surprising number of cases. Numerous men have told me that their primary reason for entering the business was to avoid the separation from their families, which an after-hours second job would require. Many women enter the business for similar reasons. Young married couples both work, and get accustomed to a double income; the wife quits her job to begin a family; and when the children come, she is reluctant to leave them to return to her former job. The solution to that dilemma might be the Amway business, which allows her to contribute to the family finances without leaving home. It was just such a motivation that led Jerry and Sharyn Webb of Texas into the business. Sharyn had two children, both under two years old, and faced the prospect of leaving them to go to work. She saw the business as an alternative. After Jerry joined her in the distributorship, they built it into a full-time income—at one time they had four children under five years old—and have become Crown Directs.

The nature of the Amway business is one which lends itself to family involvement. The corporation is fond of saying that ''Amway is a family affair,'' emphasizing that the work of the business may be a joint project by parents and children. For distributors who keep an inventory of products, there are shelves to be stocked, orders to be filled, and other small tasks that an older child can handle. The heavy emphasis on rewarding each new accomplishment, and on setting specific goals to be reached, is readily understood by children and teenagers. They learn to identify with the goals their parents set in the business.

Many families attach extra rewards for the kids—in one case, a family trip to Disney World was promised when the new pin level was reached. Smaller children seem to feel that their parents are engaged in some huge, exciting game, and they want their parents to be winners in that game. Older children understand the significance of what their parents are working for, sometimes more than the parents realize. Wally Buttrick of Michigan, then a Diamond, found his thirteen-year-old son crying one day and asked the reason. "I want you to become a Double Diamond, Daddy," he replied. "I realized then," says Buttrick, "that it was almost as important to him as it was to us." (The Buttricks reached that goal in 1978.)

It is difficult to determine to what degree this emphasis on the family was deliberately built into the Amway design. "Amway has always placed great emphasis on the family as a unit," says Rich DeVos. "We don't recruit men alone or women alone when we can recruit the entire family. From the very first, our business has been something that husbands and wives—and even children—could do together. Jay and I didn't sit down in the beginning and say, 'This is going to be a family business.' It just worked out that way. Gradually the family concept evolved, and now it is an important part of the

Amway tradition. At Amway we . . . attempt to make involvement in our business something which strengthens family ties rather than threatening them.''

Out in Morgan Hill, California, lives a young couple who
believe that Amway's attempt to nurture family togetherness
has succeeded. They are Dennis and Sharon Delisle, both of
whom came to California as children with parents who moved
West to find work. They are thirty-one years old and already
Double Diamonds. Dennis can speak of the family aspects of
the business with as much authority as anyone in Amway. He
is the son of Crown Directs Frank and Rita Delisle, and his
brother and sister-in-law, Frank, Jr., and Barbara, are
Diamond Directs. It should be underscored that these are
three *separate* distributorships; each Delisle couple has built a
business entirely on its own.

Dennis and Frank, Jr., were fourteen and sixteen when
their parents became distributors in 1962. "What I remember
most about those early days," says Dennis, "is watching
Mom and Dad work. We were the stock boys, and we used to
baby-sit the kids while Dad was holding the meetings in the
garage. We also took care of stocking the shelves. Mom and
Dad paid us fifty cents an hour, and they always included us in
what they were doing. We had a little newsletter we called the
'Chattergram'; we helped type and staple it, and the whole
family would sit around the table and put it together.''

After the elder Mr. Delisle quit his job at a print shop, he
held meetings in his garage three or four nights a week. His
children accepted the change of schedules without a mo-
ment's thought: "We were proud of Amway. Mom and Dad

100

took us back to the plant in Ada, and really made us feel like we were an important part of the business. We thought being in Amway was the most natural thing in the world.''

So natural, in fact, that both the young Delisle brothers became distributors as soon as they were old enough. Frank, Jr., became a Direct Distributor within six months; Dennis struggled for a couple of years before getting a handle on things, then became a Direct in 1967. His intention in those early days was to become an accountant and maintain a modest Amway business as a part-time business. With that in mind, he enrolled at San Jose State University with a major in accounting. He took Sharon—his girlfriend at the time—to an Amway meeting at the Masonic Temple, and signed her up as a distributor the next night. She joined, she says, just to show Dennis that she could sell at least the $100-per-month that Dennis was maintaining. She did $148 the first month; he asked her to marry him some time afterward. (Whether the two events were related is open to conjecture. Some guys will do almost anything to keep a new distributor motivated.) ''I was excited about the business. I really got caught up in the aura of it. My folks were impressed with Dennis, and they never questioned our decision to do Amway full time. There was never any fear in our minds that it wouldn't work, and I guess we communicated that confidence to them.''

By the time Dennis earned his B.S. in accounting from San Jose State, he was convinced that Amway offered him a better future than an accounting job ever could. He recalls: ''In some of my classes in college there were lots of accountants who were going to school a couple of days a week to qualify for more pay. But not one of them would get a raise of more than one hundred dollars per month, for all their hard work. I felt that if I would use that same amount of time to build my Amway business, I could become financially independent for a lifetime." So rather than take a job at graduation, he turned his full attention to his distributorship. He has never, to this day, received a paycheck from any other source.

Dennis and Sharon Delisle have two children of their own who, like their father, are growing up in the environment of an Amway family. Do they expect Annette (age five) and Dennis, Jr. (age two) to grow up loving Amway as their father did? "We sure do," says Sharon. "Mom and Dad Delisle have always loved this business. To them, the whole business was family. That's the way we want it to be for our kids. We've always been a close family, and Amway is a big part of that."

Who knows? Why shouldn't the Amway system, which has worked so well for two generations of Delisles, work again a few years later for a third?

Two thousand miles to the east, in Akron, Ohio, a similar father-son success story can be told. Jody Victor, who with his wife, Linda, is a Double Diamond, is the son of Double Diamonds Joe and Helyne Victor. As in the Delisle case, the Victors have built their distributorships independently of one another. It is another case of a bright, ambitious son successfully matching the accomplishments of an outstanding father.

Jody is thirty-one years old, and remembers the earliest days of his parents' twenty-plus years' distributorship. "Man, we had fun! We *always* had fun in this business. People used to ask me at school what my dad did for a living, and I told them he was in the business of making people happy. We were always very proud of being in Amway."

Jody was a first-grader when his father became a distributor. They lived in a small house in a working-class neighborhood. The basement was frequently under water; the furnace came up from the basement through the living room; the Victor youngsters slept in a bedroom upstairs. Jody remembers fondly the many nights that he lay awake in bed at night and listened to his father present the Amway plan to prospects in the living room below. He became a distributor as a teenager.

Soon after Jody and Linda were married, they qualified as Direct Distributors, and the very next month Jody went into the army and was sent to Fort Knox, Kentucky, for six months. He sold products around the base, used his drill sergeant's Honda to pick up and deliver them, and says he helped one entire platoon win an "honor platoon" award, thanks to his Amway shoe spray! He flew home on weekends, and with a pregnant, homebound Linda doing a giant share of the work, kept the Amway business growing.

That was in 1969. The child whom Linda was expecting is now nine-year-old Stephen. He has a younger brother and sister, and the three children call their Grandfather Victor "Poppa Amway." That affectionate label is an indication of the degree to which the Amway business pervades the life of this admirable Ohio family. "Our kids used to wonder why I don't go off to work every day like other kids' daddies," Jody says, "but now they're old enough to understand it a little better. If you ask them what they want to be when they grow up, they'll say, 'I wanna sell soap!' I'm telling you—we know a good deal when we see one in the Victor family!"

11 Escape—Alternative—Addition

"The secret to surviving is knowing what to throw away, and what to keep," says a line from a popular folk song.

For the successful Amway Direct Distributor, there comes a time of decision: to stay at the job and keep one's distributorship as a part-time income, or to leave the job and pursue the Amway opportunity on a full-time basis. It is one of those pleasant dilemmas—in either case the income is likely to be greater than in pre-Amway days—that seems difficult only to those who have to make it.

Look at the dollars: if a person with a fifteen-thousand-dollar annual income from a "regular" job builds a healthy Direct distributorship, he might make an additional fifteen thousand dollars from Amway. That's a combined income of thirty thousand dollars—not a bad improvement from pre-Amway pay. But this person reasons that the Amway income could well double or triple in a year or so, if more time were devoted to it. And there is that alarm clock to contend with every morning, and the confinement of that forty-hour week. But, on the other hand, there's a certain sense of security in a steady salary . . . . Oh, well, like the song says, life is knowing what to throw away and what to keep.

If the job is a lousy one to begin with, most people throw it away. That's what it usually comes down to—the degree of satisfaction one receives from that "regular" job. The sad fact is that most people work wherever they work to put groceries on the table. Period. A job, for most of the nearly 100 million persons in the U.S. labor force, is simply a way to make a living. For all the talk about fulfillment, sense of "calling," and love of one's profession, few people stay at a job after the financial need to be there is removed. And that is as true of Amway distributors as of the general population. The pattern of beginning the business as a part-time venture, then resigning one's job after reaching a certain level of income to go full time, is consequently a very common one. "It just doesn't make good sense," says a former engineer, "when you're making all that money and have such a pleasant life-style, to keep working at a nine-to-five grind. You may think you like your job pretty well, but when you wake up one day and realize that you don't really *have* to do it, you start planning an early resignation."

Amway as Escape. To some the decision is not a tough one at all. Some people enthusiastically dislike their jobs. For them, the freedom to punch that clock for the last time is a major goal. Kay Fletcher is a prime example. He was an engineer at Dow Chemical Company in Baton Rouge, Louisiana, with a master's degree and a young family. His job was, by many standards, a good one—but it was a job which he thoroughly disliked and wanted to walk away from. He went to his boss to resign, but lost his nerve, and was talked out of it. "I was disgusted. I lost my self-respect. For about a month, I wasn't worth shooting; I was just a big emotional mess."

After that first abortive attempt to quit, Fletcher was determined to develop such a large Amway income that he would have no second thoughts about quitting. Today, he is one of the most popular speakers on the Amway rally circuit, partially because he so forcefully expresses the common experiences of people who are trapped on a job they want to leave: "My one great goal was personal freedom," he says. "Every time I got tired, I thought about it, and it gave me a new shot of energy. It wasn't something I wanted; it was something I had to have. The day I walked off that job, I'll admit I left with mixed emotions: joy and happiness!"

Werner Gommeringer, a Canadian now transplanted in Phoenix, Arizona, also saw Amway as a means of escape. In his case, it was not so much his dislike for his job, as his feeling that it was a dead-end street, that made him look for a way out. At the age of thirty seven, he worked in the oil and gas industry in western Canada. He had worked his way up to the second-highest position in his company after nine years, when he realized that he had exhausted his potential for advancement.

"All of a sudden I woke up," he recalls. "I could see that, even though I was making more money, our standard of living was dropping each year." He and his wife, Erna, got into Amway and are now Triple Diamonds. "It's a Cinderella business," he says. "Dreams really do come true in Amway. In my old job, I used to work three days and nights without sleep, wading around in mud up to my waist. I knew I didn't want to be there when I was fifty, and, thanks to this opportunity, I won't be."

Amway as Alternative. Other people begin Amway businesses without intending to resign their other jobs, but gradually lose interest in them after achieving greater success as distributors.

Rex Renfrow from Virginia never intended to become a full-time Amway distributor when he started. He and his wife, Betty Jo, were fairly typical; they were making a good income but wanted a bit more. He was a veteran government employee, but recently has resigned his position with the Department of Agriculture, after twenty-six years, to go full time with Betty Jo as Diamonds.

Chuck Strehli got into Amway as a law student at the University of Texas. He and Jean, his wife, originally intended only to help pay bills with their part-time Amway income. Their distributorship was so successful that the legal profession lost a prospect, and Amway gained a Crown Direct. Strehli never practiced law, but stayed in Austin after finishing law school to become one of the country's top Amway leaders.

Donald Aultman, a college professor in Tennessee, began his Amway distributorship as just another business venture—he already had several—to supplement his teaching salary. First his wife, Winona, resigned her teaching job, then, as an Emerald, he followed suit. After three years he resigned at the college to go full time in Amway, "Not only because of the money, but because Winona and I are really turned on by the challenge of this business."

108

Amway as Addition. Not everyone who enters Amway succeeds, of course. And certainly not everyone succeeds at the level necessary to leave his full-time job.

Among those who do, there are many distributors who choose to maintain their ongoing professional careers. Some of the most profitable distributorships in Amway, in fact, are still operated as part-time businesses by persons who enjoy their other jobs, and have chosen not to leave them.

Tom and Carolyn Payne and Henry and Pat Crosby became friends at dental school at the University of Alabama, and developed the kind of closeness that the shared struggles of grad school sometimes produce. When the Paynes got into Amway, they wasted no time sponsoring the Crosbys, and nine years later they are Double Diamonds and Diamonds, respectively, and still close friends.

And they still practice dentistry, Payne in Alabama and Crosby in South Carolina. The payoffs of the dental profession are apparently too attractive to walk away from, at least for the time being, especially now that their larger Amway incomes enable both men to practice on a reduced schedule, without the tedium of going to the office forty-eight or fifty weeks per year.

Quite a different interweaving of Amway and professional life is managed by Ron and Dinah Stokes, both of whom work in Southern California's entertainment industry. Ron is a professional actor who has played minor roles in over one hundred television shows and numerous movies. He and Dinah have been Amway distributors since 1970, and have built an Emerald distributorship, while staying busy professionally. Work around the sound stages and back lots of Hollywood is notoriously spotty; one might work eighteen-hour days for three weeks, then do nothing at all for three weeks, while waiting for the next assignment. The self-paced nature of the Amway business makes it a perfect counterpoint to their irregular professional life, the Stokes explain, and they intend to maintain both incomes indefinitely.

There is perhaps no better example of the combination of Amway with a successful professional life than Ron and Lynne Brice, who live in a rambling, restored house in the lake country just north of Chicago. They are in their thirties, with the clean-cut, well-groomed features and fashionable wardrobes of typical upper-middle-class suburbanites. She has the stylish kind of beauty that one sees in magazines like *Vogue* and *The New Yorker*. They are Double Diamonds, with a large, active organization of distributors.

Ron is also a pilot for American Airlines, with top-notch credentials in that demanding profession. He is a 727 captain flying out of O'Hare, the nation's busiest airport. He has logged over 5 million miles in the air, and is a former vice-chairman of the local pilot's union. He was checked out as a captain at the untypically early age of twenty-eight. He is, in short, not a sometime pilot, not a marginal pilot, not an ex-pilot: He is one of the best, a veteran captain who takes a plane loaded with 127 people and jerks it into the air (well, *eases* it into the air) several times every week.

He loves it. "I take a lot of pride in flying well. If I were a co-pilot, or a flight engineer (the third man in the cockpit), I would probably have retired long ago. Sitting in that third seat and watching the guy in the pilot's seat make a decision that I would make differently would eat a hole in me. But I'm a captain, and that means I don't sit in the cockpit and watch someone else fly—I fly that thing myself, and I've never gotten over the thrill of doing that, and doing it right." Lynne—a former flight attendant—is also a licensed private pilot.

The Brices were shown the Amway opportunity by Ray Ebright, a fellow pilot with whom Ron worked on the board of the pilot's union. When Ron began trying to sponsor other people, he naturally started with other pilots because "they were the only people I knew." Several dozen pilots have become successful distributors in the last few years, though the Brices' own business has included few of them. Today, most of their Amway prospects come from casual contacts unrelated to American Airlines. He rarely tells prospects that he is a pilot "because then they want to talk about flying, and I want to talk about making money.

"I'm almost like Jekyll-and-Hyde," he told me one night as we drove through the traffic to O'Hare. "When I get to work tonight, I won't even think about the business. I'll be a pilot, and that's where my head will be. I rarely make contacts for Amway while I'm on the job, because I'm behind a locked cockpit door, so I don't interact with many people. I have lots of seniority at American, so I can pick good routes and times, go do my flying, then go home to resume building my business."

Not that he tries to keep Amway a secret from people. "When I pick a guy up in my Rolls Royce, he knows I do something besides fly airplanes," Ron grins. "We don't have to hide Amway from people, because the image of the company has become so positive, and the changes it has brought to our life-style are so obvious."

No question about that. The Brices own a home-office computer to help with their paper work; a twelve-thousand-square-foot home with lake frontage; five boats (including a sailboat, cabin cruiser, ski boat); a thirty-three-foot motor home; custom-built Excalibur for Lynne and other classic antique automobiles. And so on.

With such an immensely successful business, one wonders why Ron has continued to fly. He obviously has considered the question before: "*One,* I love to fly. *Two,* there is no good reason to quit, since Amway is designed to allow a person to do both. *Three,* I make upwards of fifty thousand dollars a year as a pilot, so why give it up?" (He is being modest; airline industry sources state that a 727 captain with fifteen years' experience, as Ron has, earns approximately seventy thousand dollars annually.) "If the person who showed us the business had said we would have to be full time, we would never have gotten in. It would have scared us to death. And that would have been a tragedy, because Amway is my major source of income now—has been for many years. The airline salary is good; but the Amway money is better."

The Brices represent that large category of Amway distributors who are successfully combining the business with another profession. They are not ordinary people, of course. The Brices are an exceptional couple, and their level of success is an exception, and not the norm, among the thousands of persons who try their hand at the business. But exceptional though they are, there are many more like them in the World of Amway: college professors, physicians, attorneys, businesspersons, engineers—all who view Amway as an addition, rather than an alternative to "that other job."

Do the Brices intend to go on flying and working Amway forever?

"Probably not," Ron responds. "One of these days, I'll retire as a pilot; but Amway I'll do from now on. As my children get older, I'd like to spend more time with them. American Airlines is a fantastic company, and they have always treated me right. But the time will come that I just want to spend more time doing what I want to do, and Amway has put me in a position to have that choice."

113

12 Pioneers

You may never meet two men more different than Dick Marks and George Halsey.

Marks is white; Halsey is black. Marks is a Canadian midwesterner; Halsey hails from the Deep South. Marks is a large man, with a strong, plainspoken manner; Halsey is small and dapper, with a soft-spoken, almost mischievous sense of humor. But for all their differences of appearance and style, Marks and Halsey share something in common: both are pioneers in the World of Amway.

There are many different kinds of pioneers. A dictionary describes a pioneer as "a person that opens or helps originate a new thought or activity or a new method or development, or . . . one of the first to settle in a new territory . . . ."

Dick Marks was a cop in midwestern Canada. He always wanted to be a cop, and wearing the blue uniform that first day on the Winnipeg Police Force was a childhood dream come true. Like many childhood dreams, this one turned out to be less exciting than it first appeared. After a few years on the force, life for Dick and his wife, Bunny, had become rather dull and unpromising, and they began looking for something else. A friend told them about Amway and tried to sponsor them. Dick was immediately negative, "That thing will never work; you should get out of it," he told the friend. So the Amway distributor—who Marks says didn't understand what the business was all about—took his advice and quit.

So much for the Dick and Bunny Marks Amway story! But about a year later, a different friend came through town from Calgary and told them about Amway. This distributor also failed to get a positive reaction from the Markses, but he had the presence of mind to leave an Amway manual behind; and the manual did what the distributor had not done—it got Dick Marks's attention. He picked up the manual and started to read it one day, and eventually decided there was something in Amway worth investigating.

So it was that when Gordon Ross offered to visit Dick and Bunny Marks and explain the full Amway system to them, they were ready. They got in, and Ross came back to show the plan to a group of prospects they invited. Only five people accepted Dick and Bunny's invitation to their first meeting. Their best friend came, but fell asleep halfway through the session. They tried again. This time thirty-seven people showed up, and they knew they were on the way. That was in the fall of 1965, and by November, the Marks had a monthly volume of eighty-seven hundred dollars, with one hundred people in their group. Dick still worked full time as a police officer; the nearest supply of products was almost one thousand miles away in Calgary; and their sponsor—the fellow who left the Amway manual with them—has never been back to see them since.

How did they make it? "We believed in it," Dick answers. "Gordon Ross showed faith in us. He convinced us that we could be successful. We'd call him on the phone and he would tell us, 'You can do it.' Every time that's what he would tell us: 'You can do it.' So we went out and did it."

The next spring, Rich DeVos came through town and stopped by to visit the Markses. He urged them to come to Grand Rapids for the Amway Convention that May. "Come on and meet the people," he suggested, "and if you don't like the meeting, you can go shopping." So they went, driving twenty-two hours in the family station wagon. What they saw opened their eyes to a bigger, wider World of Amway than they had ever imagined from their small Winnipeg distributorship. The next year they rented a bus and took forty-four of their Canadian distributors along. The next year they chartered a plane—a 100-passenger DC-6—and filled it. And the *next* year, three chartered planes were required to transport the Marks contingent to the Grand Rapids convention! "Those were important, those early trips to the national convention," Bunny recalls. "I remember seeing some of our distributors standing there in the convention, with tears running down their cheeks, they were so impressed and moved by it all. For the first time some of them really understood what Amway and free enterprise can be. It was like we all belonged to a big family."

The Marks distributorship grew steadily, at times even spectacularly. Dick resigned from the police force, not long afterward the family moved to Minneapolis, and by the late 1970s they had become, in a word, *wealthy*. In 1977, they broke new ground for Amway, achieving a level in the business never before reached, when they became Crown Ambassadors. That pin award represents the peak of the Amway system, and they will always have the satisfaction of being the first to get there. Like Mount Everest, it is there to be climbed, and others will join them there, but they were there first, and that is what being a pioneer is all about.

"If you were looking for the most perfect business in the world," Dick Marks asks, "what would it be? Write down all the qualities that are desirable in a business, and what you come up with is a description of Amway."

And how does it feel to be sitting on the very top, to have gone somewhere that nobody had been before?

"The way we look at it, we're proud of what we've achieved, but we really haven't done anything yet. We haven't even scratched the surface of the potential this business has. The best is still out there waiting for us."

George and Ruth Halsey have also broken an important barrier. They are Amway's first black Diamond Distributors. To Amway people, few honors are more coveted than membership in the Diamond Club. The group meets twice a year—all expenses paid by the company—and membership is based strictly on one's success as a distributor. The Diamond Club is a kind of informal All-Star Team, closely watched by people throughout the distributor force, with new members getting national attention. In Amway, making it really big means becoming a Diamond. Even though black distributors have been commonplace in Amway almost since its inception, none of them had ever become a member of the Diamond Club. In 1978, George and Ruth Halsey changed all that.

118

George grew up in an area of Wilmington, North Carolina, which local residents called "The Block." "They call it a ghetto now, but we didn't know that then! Life could be a little tough in The Block, and I grew up knowing that the thing you wanted to do when you lived there was to get out of there. And that meant money, which meant a good job. My mother always told me that education was the key to whatever kind of job I wanted. So I went to college."

That college was North Carolina A & T, a predominantly black university in Greensboro. He left there not only with three years of college education, but with a wife as well. Ruth was a majorette in the A & T marching band and George played saxophone when the two met during the junior year. She is one of seven children whose parents' major goal in life was a college education for their kids. After she and George were married, she began teaching school; but George began to experience the frustration so well known to ambitious young black males on the open job market in a time of high unemployment.

"I used to read those signs on some of those doors that said EQUAL OPPORTUNITY EMPLOYER," he remembers. "But when you go in there to try to get the job, you stay right where you started—at the end of the line." First he was hired to fold boxes in a pajama factory; then took work sweeping out an office building at night; and finally got a job as a policeman in the Greensboro Police Department.

He spent seven years on the force. "I was a little guy, and just about every day I had to fight. They put me walking a beat, by myself, on one of the toughest streets in town, but I earned some respect on that beat." After a few years on the force, George was told that only his lack of a college degree prevented his promotion to sergeant, so he went back to school, this time the hard way, going to classes in the daytime and walking his beat at night. He completed his degree, and still no promotion came. George began to grow disillusioned with police work.

It was not long afterward that the Halseys were introduced to Amway. George was shown the plan by "a friend of a friend." "I got interested because he told me I could make an extra four hundred dollars a month. Now, this was a white guy talking, and I didn't really know if it was just a big tale or not. But I thought I would listen to him, anyway. He gave me some cassette tapes, and that night I went to bed and listened to those tapes with an earphone plugged into my ear. That's when I started to get excited."

But not Ruth. "I just couldn't see it," she remembers. "I couldn't see it because I didn't want to see it. George got all excited, but I wasn't about to get involved in this thing. I had a big status hang-up. We weren't rich, but we sure weren't desperate. I thought I was going to have to go around knocking on doors, selling little bags of soap." Her attitude didn't begin to change, until George took her to her first rally. "I saw this man up on stage telling his story, and he started to cry. He had injured his eye mowing the lawn, and he told how the business had financed his travel to get expensive treatments. I could see he was sincere, and I began to believe in it myself."

The Halseys attacked their new business with the same drive that had already brought them from The Block to the suburbs. In the first three meetings they held, no one was sponsored. They didn't give up. George's friends at work teased him and called him "Soapy."

Ruth's fellow schoolteachers couldn't understand why she would so frequently skip lunch to take a nap, tired from late-hour Amway sessions the night before. She tried to explain that she was working for something extra, something bigger, "But they'd laugh and shake their heads. They thought I was crazy. But we had always wanted more from life, and we were working for it. We were dreamers all along. We wanted our children to have more than we had had. We worked almost around the clock. We worked all the time. And it wasn't long before our work really started to pay off. Today those other teachers are still teaching, and those other policemen are still walking that beat, but George and I are free!"

Somewhere along the way, it became important to the Halseys to succeed as an example to other black couples. "When we went on stage at a rally to receive our fifteen-hundred-dollar award, we looked around and saw that we were the only black couple on stage. We went back home determined to put it together. When I would show the plan to my friends, they looked at all those pictures in the *Amagrams,* and they would challenge me: 'Show me a black Direct.' And I finally started telling them, 'Just wait till next month, and I'll show you one, and it'll be me!' We qualified as Directs about two months later."

After less than four years, the Halseys became Diamond Directs. Their organization, though it includes distributors of both races, is largely black, and includes over forty black Direct Distributor couples. The Halsey group is a part of a larger organization, the majority of whose distributors are Deep South whites. Has that mix ever been a problem?

"Absolutely never!" George is emphatic on the point. "From the first day we got into this business, we've been treated strictly first-class. In this business, we don't care what color you are. Every time we win a new pin, we hear from our friends all over the South. They're proud of us, and we work together, we dream together, we share together completely, regardless of color. This business has changed my life. It has taught me to love people. I grew up in a time when blacks and whites would hardly speak to each other. I grew up learning to fear the white man, always afraid he was going to rip me off. But I've learned differently in Amway. This business is going to bring lots of people together. There aren't black people and white people in Amway. There are just people with dreams, that's all, and it doesn't matter what color you are, what race or creed. If you're a person with a dream, that's all that really matters!"

Halsey and Marks. Two very different couples with very different stories. Pioneers, both of them, breaking new ground in a world where only performance counts.

A pioneer is different from an explorer. A pioneer does not merely travel to new territory, as an explorer does, then return to the place whence he came. A pioneer breaks through a barrier, settles there for a while, and opens the way for others to follow. In the case of both Marks and Halsey, others are already moving into the territory which they have reached. At this writing, there is already a second Crown Ambassador, Jim and Sharon Janz of British Columbia, with others sure to get there soon. And the Halseys, newly arrived at the

Diamond Club, expect to be joined by other black distributors in that exclusive group.

If fellow policemen Dick Marks and George Halsey had ever walked a beat together, they surely would have made the most incongruous pair of cops who ever pinned on two badges. But beneath the uniform, beneath the skin, inside where it really matters, they were both dreamers, both true believers, both original, pure-bred pioneers.

13 Over There

It has been said that a successful investigative reporter must be among other things, a glutton for punishment. That thought kept coming to my mind, as I huddled in the back of an unheated taxi and stared out the window at the ice-coated city of Düsseldorf. A major winter storm was sweeping across northern Europe, and my pursuit of the "Amway experience" had unfortunately placed me squarely in the middle of it. I was trying to reach the West German village of Mettmann, just outside Düsseldorf. One taxi driver had already given up on the trip, telling me he could go no farther; but now this second, more adventurous cabbie was slowly but determinedly hauling me through the snow to Mettmann.

I had read and heard from corporate officials that one could find Amway distributors in such unlikely places as Germany and Hong Kong and Australia, but a curious writer always wants to see for himself. It was that curiosity to see a real, live, foreign distributor, operating in his natural habitat, that had brought me—frozen ears and all—to Mettmann.

Ernest Hemingway once wrote that the Germans have a

genius for irritating people—which only proves that Hemingway never met Franz and Ehrentrud Langner. They live in Mettmann, a middle-aged couple who, though already Diamond Directs in Amway, have never yet even *seen* the company's headquarters in Michigan. Franz has the look of a man of substance, with stylish, thin-rimmed glasses and dark hair graying around the temples. He wears a sweater against the winter chill and when he talks, frequently raises his forefinger upward, in the manner of a patient professor making his point to a student.

Born of East German parents, Langner moved as a young teenager to Berchtesgaden (near Munich) at the end of World War II. He worked as a young man in a textile mill, where he met Ehrentrud, a rather tall, auburn-haired young woman who worked at the same factory. After Franz and Trudy married in 1949, he attended engineering school, but found the opportunities in the textile industry in Germany disappointingly limited in the early 1950s. He looked for a way to advance. It came in the form of a job offer in South Africa, and for the next seven years the Langners lived and worked there, returning to Germany in 1960 with two sons and a valuable record of work experience as an engineer. His new job with a machine factory in Bergisch-Gladbach took him to the United States and other foreign locations on business trips, provided a middle-class income for his family, and for many years offered challenge and fulfillment for the ambitious engineer.

But gradually the Langners found themselves drifting into what, these days, is fashionably called a "mid-life crisis." By 1974 their older sons were grown and away from home. The company for which he had worked so many years had become large and impersonal, and the doors to higher positions—with correspondingly larger salaries—were firmly closed. Franz felt hemmed in; he knew he couldn't go further in his job, and he was no longer happy where he was. Trudy was feeling lonely at home, with her children grown up and no career. "She came to me one day," Franz recalls, "and asked me, 'What can I do? I feel lonely at home.' And I told her. 'There is nothing to do. We are forty-six, forty-seven years old. At this age, forget it.' Our two oldest sons were chefs, and we considered opening a restaurant, but that required capital, and we had none."

Enter Amway. A friend of Trudy's heard about a business opportunity meeting at a hotel in Bergisch-Gladbach, and asked if she would go along. "What is it?" Trudy asked. "I don't know," her friend answered, "but it sounds interesting." Franz was reluctant for the women to go alone, so he accompanied them to the meeting that night. When time came for the session to begin, no one else had shown up, so the man conducting the meeting presented the marketing plan to the three of them. The Langners found the presentation unimpressive, but decided to try the products. They ordered 760 marks (about 300 dollars at that time) worth of products and placed them all around the house, to test the reactions of their friends who would be visiting during the Christmas season. Everyone liked the products and commented on them. "Where could they be bought?" people wanted to know. Within a week all the products were gone, and the Langners ordered again and began to sell. That was the beginning of their career in Amway.

In less than four years they became Diamonds. As they got

involved more deeply in the business, the Langners met other groups in the growing German distributor force. The turning point in their business came when they traveled to Munich for a rally, and met Peter and Eva Muller-Meerkatz, a young couple who were then (as now) the fastest-growing distributors in the country. "We stayed up all night talking about Amway, arguing about the best ways to do the job, sharing our experiences. It was an exciting time for us!"

Almost all the Langners' sponsoring today is done one-on-one, frequently with prospects who have answered classified ads in the newspaper. "We emphasize the same things here that are emphasized in the United States," Langner says, "the basic ideas of doing it in the home, the simplicity of the business, and the fact that it requires little capital." Does the American identity of the business hinder their sponsoring? "Not at all! American businesses and products are everywhere you look over here, just as Volkswagen and other German products are in America. People have much respect here for American industry and marketing; and, one must remember, this is not an American business. It is Amway of Germany—it's a German business over here!"

But still the ties to the USA are strong. In Franz's office are framed photographs of DeVos and Van Andel, and on his cassette player I spotted several tapes of speeches by well-known American distributors. The Langners will travel to Ada in mid-1979, accompanied by a planeload of their distributors, to see the Amway corporate base for the first time, and get acquainted with American distributors.

Franz and Trudy Langner, like most successful German distributors, have virtually unlimited confidence in the future of Amway in their country. "We are a people who like to work," he declares, "and once we get something, we hold onto it. We are just now beginning truly to understand this business, and when we do, there is absolutely no limit to how big it might become!"

Even to a cautious person, Langner's optimistic projection seems a reasonable one. The growth chart of Amway's international operation is positive in every market area, with several countries growing at rates far above earlier corporate expectations. Australia is the oldest and most stable foreign operation. The Amway banner has flown there since 1970, and a new two-million-dollar headquarters building has just been opened in Sydney. Amway opened in Great Britain in 1973, Hong Kong in 1974, Germany in 1975, Malaysia in 1976, the Republic of Ireland and France in 1977, the Netherlands in 1978, and Japan in 1979.

Nowhere has it failed to work. That is presumably a result of careful selection of international target areas—the company would hardly go into a new country without a better-than-even chance of succeeding. Another reason for Amway's perfect batting average is apparently the unique "international sponsorship" plan which Amway has developed, by which Americans receive bonuses for the productivity of foreign distributors whom they have steered into the company. (That works for all international combinations, and European distributors are themselves sponsoring across national boundaries. Franz Langner, for example, had almost fifty Dutch distributors in his group within two months of the official opening there.) But the most important implication of Amway's success abroad is not the exceptional skill of its international staff, nor the quality of its products, nor even the cleverness of the international-sponsoring program.

A far more critical element in the formula is the sheer universality of the Amway concept. It is, after all, a concept, and not that red-white-and-blue soap box, which makes Amway unique. The Amway concept includes several key components: a chance for the little man; an unlimited ceiling on income; an emphasis on sharing rather than internal competition; a strictly performance-based reward system; public recognition for each small step of new achievement. All of that adds up to a concept called *Amway,* and one must wonder just how well such a thoroughly American concept might fit the lives of people in other countries. Is the Amway concept transportable across national boundaries? That was the question before 1970. Is it narrowly American, or might it be more universal than that? Is it basic enough to modern human experience that it can appeal to people in Germany and Japan and Malaysia?

The answer has been a startlingly emphatic *yes!*

Amway turns out to be a universal concept. It works in a variety of cultures. One gets a striking impression of the similarity, rather than the dissimilarity, of foreign distributors to their American counterparts.

A few American distributors have observed Amway's international operation at close range, by going outside the USA to build the business themselves. Among such couples are the Nellenbachs—Don and Angie—of Dublin, Ireland, from New York, by way of Birmingham, England. The Nellenbachs, who have built Direct distributorships in all three countries,

130

spearheaded the movement of the business into the Republic of Ireland.

Angie is Irish, a native of Dublin, who traveled to America as a young working girl in search of a good job and a bit of adventure. She and Don met and married in Seneca Falls, New York, and in 1966 became Amway distributors. "I met a fellow named Ron Schultz at a Knights of Columbus meeting in Syracuse," Don remembers, "and a few days later he sponsored me." The Nellenbachs became Emeralds in New York, and had a stable business there when word came that Amway was opening in England. Angie was by this time eager to move closer to Ireland; Don was ready for a change; so in 1973 they packed up and moved to Birmingham, England, to live in a country where neither had ever visited before. They had no leads, no acquaintances, nothing. Another American couple, Joe and Mary Logan, who were also building the business near Birmingham became their first and closest friends. During the early, slow days of developing a British business, the Nellenbachs lived on income from their New York distributorship. "We never stopped working with our group in New York—at least by long distance," they say today. "We still send out newsletters and performance bonus checks back to the States. That business is still as big and profitable, as when we moved away in 1973."

The Nellenbachs spent three years in England and eventually built a thriving group in the Birmingham area. They visited Angie's family often, and continually urged the British Amway staff to open the business in Ireland. "Finally they told us we could go ahead and try to get something started, but

131

that they didn't have the staff to give us any help." When
Angie's mother became bedridden with a stroke in the winter
of 1976–77, the Nellenbachs decided to move to Dublin. When
they stepped off the plane at Christmastime that winter, they
automatically became the first Direct Distributors in the Republic of Ireland.

"Coming in here was a real challenge. We made arrange-
ments to have products shipped in from England and began
holding meetings immediately. We started with Angie's family
and branched out from there." In the two years since the
Nellenbachs arrived in Dublin, they have broken off two Direct Distributors and maintain a Ruby-level volume in their
personal group.

"We've done in two years here what it took us five years to
do in England," Don says. "This difference is mostly us—
England is really booming lately—but Amway certainly has a
great potential in Ireland. People are still warm and friendly
here; they still go and visit each other in their homes. Dublin is
a great place to live and a great place to build an Amway
business."

No argument there. From all the evidence, Dublin seems to
be a perfectly suitable place to make the Amway concept
work. Just like Mettmann, West Germany; and Chicago; and
Marseilles, France; and Tokyo, and Adelaide, Australia; and
Hong Kong, and Kuala Lumpur, Malaysia; and Kansas City,
and on and on and on . . . .

14 Aristocrats

Stan Evans is an aristocrat.

He may not fit your image of one—certainly not if you think of an aristocrat as a European blue blood, a member of a royal family, born to wealth and privilege.

In the old days, the aristocracy was that privileged few, that small circle to whom came all the wealth, the fame, the power. No one ever cracked that group. Aristocrats were aristocrats because of birth. If you were born a peasant, you remained a peasant. No amount of ambition, skill, sacrifice, or hard work would ever change a peasant into an aristocrat.

The coming of democracy changed all that. It swept aside the old aristocracy of birth and bloodlines, and established in its place a new aristocracy of achievement. In this new order, the aristocrats are the achievers, the dreamers, the winners. Today, a man can be either an aristocrat or a bum—it's entirely up to him. The circle of privilege and power was thrown open to any person who could win it. In an aristocracy of achievement, a man can be born of poor parents, unknown to

133

the world, and rise to the councils of the mighty. By main force, he can make himself an aristocrat.

In the novel *Ragtime,* a character is described in this manner: "He did not believe in aristocracy except that of the individual effort and vision." If there is any single description that would fit all Amway winners, this is it. The heart of the Amway system is its belief in an aristocracy based solely on "individual effort and vision." By that definition, Amway is a company of true aristocrats.

Cowboy. Stan Evans is one of them. He was a cowboy—an honest-to-goodness, real, live cowboy—before Amway changed his life. He worked with his father on a Nebraska ranch. They worked three thousand acres, rode the range, mended fences, raised beef cattle from a two-hundred-head breeding herd. He married Ruth when he was twenty-two, and they lived the demanding life of the ranch for the next seven years. Gradually they became discontented. They wanted land of their own and wondered if they would ever accumulate the money to get it. It is said that farmers live poor and die rich. For Stan and Ruth, that didn't sound very attractive.

While in Denver for a bull sale, the Evanses saw the Amway plan. They decided to try it, but "didn't really think we could do it out here. We could see how maybe it would work in the city." One must understand that "out here" means Haigler, Nebraska. Population: 240. (All of Dundy County has less than 3,000 people.) Let me tell you exactly what there is to see in beautiful downtown Haigler: one grocery store, a beer joint, one liquor store, one filling station, a hardware store, one small post office, and a barber shop with a single chair. That's it, folks. No way to build an Amway business at a jumping-off place like Haigler, right?

Wrong. The Evanses are fighters. They are workers. They sponsored "everybody in sight." Nine months after they got in, they went to Stan's father and resigned from the ranch. Less than two years later, they were Diamond Directs. Today they are Triple Diamonds; Stan has served as president of the board of the Amway Distributor's Association; and they can afford the life-styles of middle-class jet-setters on the income from their Amway business.

Not to be misleading, I must report that small-town-boy Stan Evans has fled Haigler to live amid the bright lights and hustle-bustle of a larger city. His present home: Wray, Colorado, just down Highway 34 about 17 miles from Haigler. Population: 2,000.

Courage. Curtis and Virginia Ledbetter know something about moral courage. They have proved twice that when they genuinely believe in something, they have the courage to act on it.

The first challenge was a matter of religious faith. Curtis was a chaplain, with a rank of major, in the U.S. Air Force. An ordained minister, he was on duty at the Air Force Academy in Colorado Springs when he and Virginia converted to the Church of Jesus Christ of the Latter Day Saints (Mormons). Becoming Mormons required a major sacrifice for them: a military regulation requires any chaplain who changes religious affiliation to resign his commission and leave the chaplaincy. They weighed the costs, then took the step.

Curtis went back to grad school, earned a doctorate in educational psychology, and joined the faculty at Brigham Young University in Orem, Utah. They became absorbed in the life of the Mormon church.

It was Virginia who first saw the Amway opportunity, and she went home convinced it was for them. Curtis had no idea what it was all about, but agreed to trust her judgment and try it. Of the first twenty-three couples they showed the business to, only two decided to join them. They persisted. "We had a dream," Virginia says. "We wanted to be able to support our sons in full-time missions work. We wanted to give more money to the church and still have a secure, financial future. When we saw the plan explained, we saw hope and opportunity that we hadn't had before, and that kept us working."

The Ledbetters are Diamonds today. Curtis still teaches at Brigham Young ("I look at it as a call. It's exciting work. I want to be able to do it for nothing."), but his Amway income is several times larger than his professor's salary. "All I have to do," he says, "is look at my wife and five children, and I see six reasons for being in this business. That's enough for me."

Jet-Jockey. Lew Riggan is a Texan who likes to make money. He grew up poor, so he knows what it's like, and he has decided to avoid being that way again. "My dad was a laundry-truck driver," he says, "and he put in me a desire to get ahead. I'm proud of that, and I'm proud of him. But I've never had any doubt that I would have something better."

Riggan spent eleven years in the U.S. Air Force, before resigning to become a pilot for American Airlines. The money was good, but money is never quite good enough, it seems, so

Lew looked for ways to make additional income on the side. As an investor, he made a good pilot. First he lost four thousand dollars in the stock market. Then he lost another four thousand dollars in dry oil wells. Then he bought a ten-acre grapefruit grove and lost eight thousand dollars there. Next he bought a laminating machine, then some old duplexes: zero again.

About that time, along came Amway. John Newberry, another pilot, showed him the plan and sponsored him. He had finally found an investment—of effort, this time, and not money—that would pay off for him. It was the second-best thing that ever happened to him.

The first-best thing was a beautiful fashion coordinator named Darlene. She was single, living in Dallas, when she became a distributor in Lew's organization. He held her first meeting for her, and six months later they were married. Their honeymoon was spent on the *Enterprise,* Amway's yacht. (Lew now talks with great authority when he discusses the various rewards of the business.)

The Riggans are now Double Diamonds, and still live in the Dallas area.

Out of the Rain. I met a man once who is a Crown Direct in Amway simply because he had sense enough to get in out of the rain!

His name is Dallas Beaird. Dallas and his wife, Betty, live in a posh suburban neighborhood just outside Los Angeles. Their home is worth a trip to West Covina to see. It is 6,300 square feet of sheer luxury: sauna, heated pool, shuffleboard courts, sun deck, sunken living room, and two wet bars, where the teetotaling Beairds serve lots of fresh fruit drinks. If the Beairds ever get tired of it, they can always head for their other house in El Monte, or their vacation home on Lake Arrowhead—when they aren't traveling around the world, which they recently did. (It's enough to make a fellow want to be a Crown!)

Beaird was in the construction business with his two brothers when he saw the Amway plan. They had a big company, with one hundred men and three million dollars under contract at one time. They built many churches—over thirty of them—and were building a Methodist church in Downey when they got into Amway, sponsored by his brother.

Soon afterwards, it started raining and rained for three solid weeks. Very unusual for Southern California. With nothing to do but watch the rain, Dallas spent those three weeks "trying out the business," while waiting to get back to his construction project. That three weeks taught him something. "Things were really rolling along by then. We became Direct a few months later, the same month I finished the church building. "So, I just didn't take any more contracts," Dallas explains. "By the time I finished that contract, we were so busy with this business, we just kept going with it."

You bet they did. All the way to Crown.

Burn, Baby, Burn. Bob Crisp never flickers. He never smolders. He always burns. The word *intensity* was invented to describe guys like Bob Crisp. He is a young, aggressive, tightly wound Double Diamond, who never met a job he didn't think he could handle. And he's usually right.

When Bob and his wife, Jo, became Amway distributors in 1975, he was already a dazzlingly successful insurance agent, writing over $15 million in policies in a five-year period. This was in Tulsa, Oklahoma, where the Crisps lived with five children, including three-month-old twins. That size family hardly leaves room for a part-time job, but Jo was ready to tackle Amway if Bob was. "I was excited about getting into a business Bob and I could do together," she says. "But I was also a little frightened. And I was determined to do whatever I had to do to pull my share of the load."

So they began. It took eight months for them to reach Direct, which by Bob's standards was too slow. So they felt around for high gear, found it, and have grown at a phenomenal rate since. Twenty-two months later they were Diamonds; a year after that they were Double Diamonds.

Bob Crisp with a microphone is like Al Hirt with a trumpet; he feels at home and so does the microphone. He is direct and articulate, and he always knows what he came to say: "I believe you have to burn. You have to be two hundred and twelve degrees. You have to be steam. When I first got into Amway, I wondered 'What does it take to really do this business?' I decided it was belief, and when we became true believers, we really began to grow."

No one doubts that Bob and Jo Crisp believe. If you can't tell by looking in his eyes, you can tell by looking at his sales!

Missionary. Bob Schmidt. When he talks, the words are like a Canadian blizzard—they fly so thick, I can never quite listen as fast as he talks. But then I'm a southerner, and he is from the plains of Saskatchewan. Born and raised. He and his wife, Joyce, were high-school friends in western Canada, and as teenagers were both committed members of the Mennonite church.

So when Bob left high school, he went directly to Africa—the Congo—for a two-year duty as a missionaries' aide. He lived out in the bush, near the Angola border, with a co-worker named Bernie, and the two of them were evacuated by U.S. military forces when savage fighting swept the country following independence in 1960. Ten years later he went back, this time with Joyce as his wife, for another assignment in what is now called Zaire. They worked in the town of Kananga, producing Protestant religious materials in the Tshiluba language.

After four years, Bob Schmidt came home: he was fifty pounds lighter, sick with ulcerative colitis, and was sent home to stay. In 1975 Bob and Joyce saw Amway. They took to it like a kid takes to an ice-cream cone. "For the first time in our married life we saw something that we could do together." Bob held two meetings the very first night he showed the plan, one at 5:30 and one at 8:30. He has barely slowed down since. He and Joyce now are Double Diamonds and live in Vancouver, British Columbia.

Try to talk to Bob about himself, and you usually hear instead about Jim Janz—the personable Vancouver Crown Ambassador who has been his mentor in the business—or one of the distributors in his group. He is constantly redirecting the spotlight away from himself, and toward someone else. What about *you*, Bob? "I've never felt as complete a person as I have since Amway. It's touched every part of my life. What else can I say?"

That says it very well.

Southern Style. The Deatons are all southern charm and hospitality. Dorsey is a college professor with a Ph.D. from Emory University; Pam is a psychiatric counselor with a master's degree. When you hear people talking about the young, progressive, new-look southerners of Atlanta, Georgia, it is people like the Deatons that they are talking about.

After years of paying tuition and grad school bills, the Deatons needed more money than their salaries provided. "We had an education, but no life-style to go with it," Dorsey recalls. In 1966 there was good news and bad news: the good news was that they received a forty-thousand-dollar inheritance that year; the bad news was that they lost it all in the stock market. *All* of it. In an attempt to recoup their losses, they borrowed more money and "went for the home run," as they describe it. Within six months that investment had ended in bankruptcy. "We lost the inheritance, had our nest egg wiped out, and went into hock," all within six months.

"We were disillusioned and very cynical about financial things," they say. It was against that backdrop that the Deatons first saw Amway. On a trip to Texas, they visited one of Pam's old high-school friends and were shown the plan. Pam wanted to get in, and said so that night. "Not me," answered Dorsey. "You can do it if you want to, but not me. I didn't get my Ph.D. to be an Avon lady." They signed up the next morning.

Today, nine years later, they are Double Diamonds, busily

141

involved in their booming business and their plans for a custom-built dream house near Atlanta. "Our friends were reluctant to show us the business because they thought we weren't 'the type,' " Pam recalls.

"And I agreed with them," Dorsey joins in.

Obviously, Pam knew something he didn't know. And Dorsey has been happily proving himself wrong ever since.

Born to Teach. Ask a computer for a profile of the perfect teacher, and what you get is Roland Hughes. He is the consummate teacher: patient, intelligent, with an air of calm authority. Watch Roland Hughes with a piece of chalk in his hand, and you say that this guy was born to teach.

A native Pennsylvanian, Roland met and married Molly, a beautiful South Carolinian with a fine sense of style in dress as well as in living. After earning a doctorate from the University of Pennsylvania of the prestigious Ivy League, Roland moved to the University of South Carolina and earned a tenured position there. "I loved teaching," he remembers, "but I eventually grew frustrated with the bureaucratic part of the university life." It was about that time that he was shown the Amway plan, in late 1972.

Roland and Molly took to Amway as naturally as—well, as naturally as a gifted teacher picks up a piece of chalk. They are Diamond Directs today, still in South Carolina, though no longer at the university. "I *teach* the business," Hughes says. "I see it as an opportunity to teach and counsel, and I've done more of that in this business than I ever did in my other profession."

Happiness is being paid well for doing something one truly enjoys.

15 Smorgasbord

Questions. I get questions. When you write a book about something, you are constantly asked to explain it, or at least describe it, to all manner of people with all manner of notions about the subject. So I get questions about Amway. What kind of persons are in Amway, they want to know, and why do they get in, and what do they get out of it, anyway?

Mostly the questions are about the people. An editor in New York once wrote to me regarding Amway people: "I am amazed at the effect Amway has on its distributors. One keeps asking oneself, 'Why would someone like that want to do something like this?' " For some reason, many outsiders think of Amway distributors as being a distinguishable type, a *species*. It is a glaring misconception.

Amway is a smorgasbord of persons. Its rich pluralism is part of its mystique—and, no doubt, also part of its great vitality.

Who succeeds in Amway?

Old people and young people and in-between people. There is a Direct couple in Belfast, Ireland, who are eighty-six and eighty-three years old. Ann Powers of Florida went to her new-Direct seminar at the age of seventy. I have also met couples who have become Directs in their teens—including a nineteen-year-old rice farmer and his eighteen-year-old wife from a town with the memorable name of Weiner, Arkansas.

Religion? Makes no difference. Directs may be Protestants, Jews, Catholics, or nothing at all. There is a large group of Mormon distributors in Utah; I have spoken with Buddhist distributors in Los Angeles; and once I met two men in Pittsburgh who told me they were Black Muslims.

Education doesn't seem to matter, either. Some of the favorite stories in Amway folklore are of men like Charlie Marsh, who with his wife, Elsie, became Amway's first Crowns. Despite dropping out of school in the ninth grade, they have succeeded as grandly as any distributors, ever. Nor is there an absence of Ph.D.'s, M.D.'s, and virtually every other type of college degree.

What about geography? Are successful Amway people more likely to be found in one place than in another? Apparently not. There are Directs in all fifty states, in towns with names like Red Deer and Issaquah and Stink Creek. Yet in big Eastern cities, such as Boston and Baltimore, Amway rallies draw crowds of several thousand distributors.

Occupations? Take your pick, and somewhere there is an Amway Direct who represents that way of earning a living. In addition to the conventional categories, I have talked with Directs whose unusual occupations range from a portable outhouse salesman, to a Las Vegas showgirl, to pro-football player offensive lineman Dave Taylor, who draws one paycheck from the Baltimore Colts for knocking people down

144

on a football field, and earns another by teaching them to get on their feet again in something called Amway.

Does social background make a difference? Decide for yourself: I had coffee one night with Diamond Directs Robert and Margaret Echols. He is a former welder, who spent his pre-Amway days working in the oil fields of East Texas, riding in rodeos for a few dollars, always making a living with his hands. With him that night was one of the Directs in his group: Lenny Kacenjar, who is concertmaster and first violinist for the Shreveport Symphony Orchestra, and a graduate of the high-brow Juilliard Conservatory in New York City.

On a different occasion, I ate lunch with a Harvard University administrator who was "learning the ropes" in Amway from a former waitress.

Bill Britt once held an opportunity meeting into which walked a "scraggly-looking fellow" with shoulder-length hair, an Indian headband, glassy-eyed look—all the marks of a confirmed hippie. After the session, he walked around and around the blackboard, muttering, "Man, that's cool." To Britt's surprise, he got into the business; and, three years later, that distributorship which he represented is still a large, secure Direct leg. Does pre-Amway life-style matter? It surely doesn't seem to.

What about population density? Does that factor limit how well the business can grow? Consider this: in a place called White Horse, in the Yukon Territory of Canada near the Arctic Circle, there are at least five Silver Producers. One lady there became a Direct Distributor living fourteen kilometers from town. In contrast, there is a single ward (about ten city blocks) in a town in Utah with two Diamonds, one Emerald, one Pearl, two Ruby Directs, and one Direct. Brian Hays, a Double Diamond from Chicago, once told me that in a single Bible-study class at his church there is a Ruby, an Emerald, a Double Diamond, and another Ruby who sponsors a Diamond.

The speed with which the business is built varies widely, too. A couple in Montreal recently became Direct Distributors after ten years in the business, while there are several cases of persons becoming Directs in their first month. In one example, a California distributor had a sales volume of $7,851 in his first 19 days in the business.

Amway is a smorgasbord. All kinds of people from all kinds of places. And they get into the business for all kinds of reasons.

Money, of course, is the main reason. But it isn't quite as simple as all that, even if money is at the root of most decisions originally. There are as many reasons to get into Amway as there are people involved. Consider these:

- Agnes Hill was a sixty-year-old distributor who wanted merely to make enough money to keep from losing her home. (She made that, and more. Now an Emerald.)
- André Blanchard, a Triple Diamond from Quebec, originally got in so he could quit one of his two jobs—working as a shoe clerk on weekends for sixty dollars per month. All he wanted was to spend weekends at home with his wife.
- Paul Freehling got in just to keep an Amway distributor friend from getting angry with him. He and his wife, Nancy, are Emeralds today.
- James Meredith, the famous civil-rights leader, got in and became a Direct in order to have a solid economic opportunity to show to lower-class Mississippi black friends.

146

- Bob Andrews in Florida got into the business with one of his former schoolteachers. His goal: to make $73.50 a month for a monthly Chevelle payment, "so my Dad would give his blessings to my wedding plans."
- A father and his grown daughter in Alabama joined Amway together, shortly after his divorce, to give them a project which they could share, which would be unaffected by their difference in age.
- The Fred Baldwin family from Connecticut used their Amway business to enable them to leave the corporate rat-race and operate an old country inn in Chester, Vermont.
- Clayton Overton, a California M.D., who is a Diamond, joined Amway to help offset the soaring cost of malpractice insurance for his medical practice.
- Carl and Sue Mackey came into the business while he was a submarine officer in the U.S. Navy. Sue was from New York, the daughter of a successful Manhattan executive. She had an unhappy childhood which had left her embittered, carrying emotional scars from a home with too much money and too little love. What made her decide that Amway was for them? "I saw a lot of people in this business with a lot of money," she says. "But they had more happiness, more fulfillment than I had ever seen in my life. I never saw these folks drunk; I never heard them swear; I never heard them get rude with each other; I never saw them make passes at each other; I never heard the women condemning their husbands. It was a whole different world. I said to Carl, 'Babe, if we can have money, and live like that, let's have a go at it.' "

And they did, of course. Carl eventually left the navy (after seventeen years), and they are now Emerald Directs in Washington.

147

They get in for all kinds of reasons. And once they get in, they make all kinds of mistakes, and run into all manner of obstacles: like Willis Coleman, now a Double Diamond, who bought seventeen dozen doughnuts, perked sixty cups of coffee, and set up twenty-five borrowed folding chairs at his house for his first Amway meeting. One person showed up.

. . . or Jack and Eileen Barker of British Columbia. While they were qualifying as Directs, they learned he had cancer of the throat and couldn't speak for several weeks—and she broke her leg. Their apartment was at the top of a fifty-step flight of stairs. Still they sponsored people. She lay on the sofa and explained the plan, while he stood at the chalkboard and diagrammed her talk. They qualified.

. . . Leo and Amy Grant from Utah. When they first began speaking before crowds, he was so shy that they held hands behind the podium—he would talk until running out of something to say, then would squeeze Amy's hand; then she would talk until he was sufficiently composed to resume, then another squeeze, and so on. It was with this "system of alternating squeezes" that they overcame their stage fright—and became Diamond Directs.

Where do they find people to sponsor?

That question I get frequently from people who can't imagine how one could possibly round up enough prospects to make the system work. The answer: everywhere and anywhere.

Joseph Billo, who attended the Harvard School of Business, got several prospects by placing an ad in the Harvard Alumni Magazine. I met a medical doctor who was sponsored by Bob Chadsey, a garbage collector—and both became Direct Distributors. Gerry Herrera in Puerto Rico sponsored his dentist and helped him become an Emerald. Jerry and Sharyn Webb were sponsored by the people from whom they rented their apartment. I met an enlisted man in the Canadian Air Force who was sponsored by one of his officers while on duty in Moose Jaw.

And then there is the case of Charlie and Jennie Cormier of Massachusetts. They *asked* to be sponsored—by an elderly gentleman who delivered their milk. They had heard about the business, knew their milkman was a distributor, and asked him to show them the plan. But when he came to do so, he merely read to them from the manual, and Charlie fell asleep during the ordeal. They got in anyway. They became Direct Distributors in ten months; Charlie quit his job as an IBM service representative six months later; and they eventually became Diamonds.

What do they get from the business?

Well, money. And all the things money can buy. But they get other things, too—lots of other things—of the sort that money cannot buy.

Dexter and Birdie Yager are Triple Diamonds whose financial benefits from the business have been immense. But more important, they say, have been the intangible rewards—the personal growth, the sense of pride in what they have accomplished, and most especially the positive relationships with other Amway people. "Becoming Directs was a thrill for us," Yager says, "but it wasn't nearly as exciting as when we helped that first couple in our group to become Directs. We were so happy for them, we just sat down in the living room and bawled.''

It is interesting that when distributors talk about the things they have received from the Amway experience, it is that kind of reward which is mentioned more often than the financial kind.

Maybe Ron Boyanovsky said it best. He's a Diamond from Oregon, so he ought to know something about what people get from Amway. "So many people have lost the *romantic* aspect out of their lives," he says, "and this business puts it back in again."

16 Where Have All the Heroes Gone?

It was during a Boston-to-Los Angeles flight, sitting by the window of a DC-10, looking down at the flat farmland of the Midwest, that I first realized how completely I had come to admire the people and principles of the "Amway experience."

I was reading a book titled *Heroes* by another young writer, Joe McGinnis. What I was reading bothered me. McGinnis was writing not about heroes, but about the absence of heroes. There aren't any more heroes, he was saying. They're all gone. Everywhere he looked, the people who ought to be heroes had feet of clay right up to their hips. "The truth was," he concluded, "we did not have heroes any more because there were no heroic acts left to be performed."

I laid the book aside and stared out the window to think about what I had read. I disagreed with him. *Though he argues his case well, he is wrong,* I thought. Though he shows many so-called heroes to be bums and worse, he still is wrong about there being no more heroes. *He was wrong because he was looking in the wrong places, looking at the wrong people,*

151

I thought. And to provide evidence for that view, I began to search through my own memory to find heroes there; people whom I knew to live lives of heroic quality; people to admire and emulate. I turned inside my own head to find such people, and I found . . . Amway people!

When that awareness hit me, it was almost startling. *Whom do I know,* I asked myself, *whose example I would offer to my children? Whose qualities, or courage makes my own blood run a little faster, make me want to stretch a bit more in the direction of my own potential.* And when I scanned my own mental list, it was dotted with . . . Amway people!

Henry Fairlie is a journalist who wrote recently about heroes in *Harper's Magazine:*

> A society . . . or an individual . . . that has no heroes will soon grow enfeebled. Its purposes will be less elevated; its aspirations less challenging; its endeavors less strenuous . . . . Heroes are against things-as-they-are . . . . To talk of heroes is to talk of ourselves, of our own aspirations and endeavors to realize them, of what we expect of ourselves . . . if we no longer have any heroes, it may be not because no one is fit to be a hero, but because we are not fit to recognize one. Individuals without heroes do not want to be told of men and women whose example might disturb them, calling them to effort and duty and sacrifice or even the chance of glory.
>
> (from "Too Rich for Heroes"), November 1978

Amway is a peculiar slice of the world in which heroes are still fashionable. That may not be so much because its people are so heroic, but because they are willing to recognize and salute the heroism in one another. And that is itself an uplifting and ennobling quality. Cynicism is an easy trait to learn. Develop a condescending smirk; learn to snicker at the sight of an honest tear; and declare that all people are frauds, and most especially those who profess to believe in goodness. Being a cynic is easy, but also terribly impoverishing.

Much better to allow ourselves a bit of honest admiration for the person who has something we want, who has it because he worked for it—and to use his example as a motivating influence for ourselves. That is the kind of healthy hero-worship one finds in Amway. It is neither the negativism of looking at people with basic distrust, nor is it the mindless celebrity-worship of those who try merely to feed off someone else's success. It is a balance that allows us, without self-consciousness, to say about another person, "There goes a person whose qualities I admire and emulate."

Dan Williams, a Crown Direct who is himself a symbol of extraordinary accomplishment, once told an Amway crowd: "Don't look to individuals in the business as your examples—but to the principles which they demonstrate. Embrace their qualities. The person is just a person. He's just human. But look at the things he has done that make him admirable, and be willing to believe in those things."

Jay Van Andel and Rich DeVos are heroes—not just to Amway distributors, but to many other people who value the traits which they embody, and who seek the things which they have achieved. They give other people hope, and that is a pretty rare thing these days. They give people an example to aspire to, and a set of principles to try to live up to. They may resist the idea; they may not wish the burden of such a role;

153

but it is there nonetheless, and they have learned to wear it with grace.

And there are others like them. People who, though flawed, are yet admirable at the core, and who in some particular detail of character set a standard for others. That may be a limited definition of heroism, but it is an honest one. It allows men and women to draw strength from one another without abandoning a sense of proportion about it all.

"There is evidence that everyone is capable of his own peculiar heroism," wrote Irving Stone. "He may not recognize it under that imposing title, for he is merely doing what his instincts tell him he must do to set his life straight; yet it is, in fact, so great a heroism that his neighbor, living out his own unrecognizable heroism, is awestricken at the other man's courage: and that is what holds the world together."

If that is true of the world at large, it is doubly true of the World of Amway. For in Amway, individual heroism is identified, called by its name, and held aloft for all to see. There are still winners, still champions, still heroes in the World of Amway, for the simple reason that the people themselves do not flinch from having it so. Amway still dares to draw a *winner's circle,* to draw the line sharply and clearly, and to say to all winners: "Step inside. This place is for you. Not because of your name or title or station in life; not because of your color of skin or social class. This place is for you because you earned it. You won it. You have made yourself a winner, and the winner's circle is where you deserve to be!"

Glossary

What is an Amway distributor, and what does one do?

Basically, Amway distributors do two things: They sell
Amway products to their friends, neighbors, and other retail
customers—and they recruit other people to do the same.

Selling the products is simple. The distributor has a product
list of over 150 items to offer the customer. These products are
made by Amway, usually come in concentrated form, and
most are everyday items for home and personal care that
everyone uses. The distributor makes an immediate income
on all the products he sells, usually about 30 percent of the
retail price.

The second activity—that of *recruiting* other people to become distributors—is called "sponsoring." Under some con-
ditions, the distributor may receive a bonus on the sales volume of anyone he brings into the business. There is no money
to be made merely for recruiting a new distributor, but if that
distributor actually goes to work and generates sales, the
company pays a bonus to the sponsor for supplying him with

products and training him in sales techniques. One can make a potentially large income if there are large numbers of people working actively in the Amway business whom he or she has sponsored.

Successful Amway *distributors* are constantly working not only to sell products themselves, but to urge other people to "go thou and do likewise." Amway operates a string of warehouses around the country called *Regional Distribution Centers,* and products are shipped from these points to the distributors, who take them personally to the customer. It is strictly a cash-as-you-go proposition; the customer pays cash to the distributor, and the distributor pays cash to the company.

The World of Amway has its own vocabulary, parts of which are as understandable as Chinese to someone not privy to the jargon. For the uninitiated reader, here is a quick and handy Amway Glossary:

Sponsor To "sponsor" another individual is to bring him into the business by persuading him to sign an application and become a distributor himself. *A* receives no money for sponsoring *B*, but agrees to train, supply, and motivate him (or her), and receives a bonus from the corporation based on *B*'s sales volume, as *B* actually develops the business.

Leg Every new distributor whom *A* sponsors becomes a "leg" in his organization. When *A* sponsors *B*, *B* is one of his legs, along with anyone whom *B* might ultimately sponsor. So the number of legs *A* has is the same as the number of people he has personally sponsored.

Personal group   All the distributors whom *A* has sponsored, plus those whom *they* have sponsored, and so on, down to the first Direct Distributor. To say that *X* is in *A*'s "personal group" doesn't mean that *A* is his boss, or any such thing as that. It simply means that *X* is somewhere in the "family tree."

Direct Distributor   Becoming a Direct Distributor is the first major goal in the Amway business. That level is reached when a distributor and his or her group generate sales of approximately eight thousand dollars per month for three straight months. (The exact dollar amount changes, as it is periodically adjusted for inflation.) When *A* becomes a Direct Distributor, he purchases his products directly from the corporation, rather than from his sponsor.

Show the plan   To "show the plan" is to explain the Amway sales and marketing plan to a prospect. *A* may show the plan with the use of a blackboard, slides, flip chart, or simply by telling the prospect how the system works.

Sponsoring meeting   Any meeting in which a distributor brings a number of prospects together to show the plan to all of them simultaneously.

Break off a Direct   When *A* sponsors *B* into the business, and *B* reaches the level of a Direct Distributor, *A* is said to have "broken off a Direct Distributor." In other words, he has helped a distributor whom he sponsored to reach the level of Direct Distributor. The corporation pays a monthly bonus to *A* for every person he breaks off, based on 3 percent of the new Direct's volume.

Pin awards   Amway has a series of pins which are awarded to Direct Distributors who continue to increase their businesses. These pins indicate roughly how big *A*'s volume has become, and the size of his income. The pin awards, in ascending order, are as follows: RUBY, PEARL, EMERALD, DIAMOND, DOUBLE DIAMOND, TRIPLE DIAMOND, CROWN, CROWN AMBASSADOR.

Conventions   The company holds dozens of conventions and rallies each year, ranging in size from very small meetings to the 30,000-plus who attended a Washington, D. C., rally in 1975. Each fall, the company celebrates Free Enterprise Day, with an estimated 140,000 people attending 140 simultaneous rallies across the country.

Home Office   The home-office operation at Ada—the Center for Free Enterprise—includes the executive office area plus displays explaining the free-enterprise system, an auditorium, an Amway Museum, and portrait sculptures of the founders, which were placed there by the distributors themselves. The Ada facility employs plant workers, chemists and scientists in the research and development laboratories; computer experts to run the IBM 3033 computer and other high-speed processing equipment; a legal staff of attorneys; printers to operate the huge presses in the printing plant; artists and photographers in the graphic-arts studio; and many other persons with specialized skills. Amway makes its own cardboard boxes and plastic bottles, shoots its own commercial photography, and prints its own containers, labels, and sales material.

A fleet of tractor-trailer rigs hauls products to the regional warehouses, aided by red-white-and-blue Amway railway cars. The aviation department employs ten pilots and five mechanics to operate the company's two BAC 1-11 jets and 2 smaller Cessna jets. The two larger planes are similar, with plush custom-made interiors. Each carries 25 passengers and a crew of 3, flies 500 miles per hour at altitudes up to 39,000 feet, and travels an average of 400,000 miles per year, taking Amway executives and distributors around the country. And there is the corporate diesel yacht, the *Enterprise,* a 116-foot vessel that sleeps eight guests (plus crew) and serves as a "floating conference center" for top-performing distributors.

All the facilities, hardware, and staff of the Amway home office in Ada have the task of helping the distributors in the field build stronger, more profitable businesses. What is good for the distributors is good for Amway. Amway products are not sold in supermarkets or drugstores, and the corporation therefore depends on the distributor force to market everything it produces. It is a good arrangement, because it demands that corporate leaders work constantly to help the distributor be more productive. "The corporation at Ada is the heart of Amway, but we are the blood," one distributor described it.

To keep that "blood" pumping, the company maintains a large number of services to help distributors build their businesses. An audiovisual department produces cassette tapes and 16-mm films explaining the Amway opportunity. A virtual flood of printed material is mailed—over seven million copies of the monthly magazine *Amagram* go out per year, and other materials are printed in English, Spanish, French, German, Dutch, Japanese, and Chinese. Contact with the distributor force is also maintained by the work of an aggressive group of young men and women with an appetite for the road, who conduct some 150 rallies and seminars around the country each year. The corporation also has a limited program of consumer advertising in the national media: ads in magazines such as *Time, Newsweek,* and *Ebony;* television spots on ABC and NBC's evening news; and on the Mutual Broadcasting System as well as on Paul Harvey's radio-news show.

The company provides other services to the distributor force which are not directly related to the business itself. An example is the Amway Mutual Fund, which is a professionally managed investment company in which many distributors have invested. Through their membership in the Amway Distributors Association, they can also participate in group medical insurance programs. (This Glossary is adapted from chapter 4 "The Plan" in *The Possible Dream.*)